More Than Money

The Hidden Rules of Wealth, Happiness, and Freedom That Schools Never Teach You

Copyright

For permission requests, write to the publisher at: swifttechnologydev@gmail.com

Table of Contents

PART I – STORIES THAT SHAPE OUR FINANCIAL BEHAVIOR

INTRODUCTION

Why We Get Money Wrong

If you ask ten people what money means to them, you'll get ten different answers.

For some, it's safety.

For others, it's freedom.

For many, it's stress.

We like to think that money is about math—spreadsheets, budgets, percentages, and formulas. And yes, the numbers matter. But the truth is that money has far less to do with numbers than we like to believe. It has more to do with how we feel.

If money were only about math, then nobody would have credit card debt. No one would gamble away their savings. No one would panic-sell at the bottom of a market crash or buy a car they can't afford just to impress people they don't even like.

Instead, most of our decisions with money are shaped by emotions: fear, greed, envy, pride, hope. They are shaped by the stories we tell ourselves—stories built from where we grew up, what we've experienced, and who we want to become.

This book is about that.

The Invisible Hand of Experience

Imagine two people.

One was born in 1950. Their parents remembered the Great Depression; they grew up watching newsreels about rationing, layoffs, and runaway inflation. Saving and security became their default setting.

The other was born in 1995. They grew up during decades of steady growth, low inflation, rising home values, cheap credit, and tech billionaires who became rich overnight. Risk, to them, feels normal. Volatility looks like opportunity.

Both are smart. Both can read the same financial book. But they will behave completely differently with their money—because their experiences shaped their beliefs long before a spreadsheet ever did.

When we talk about money, we think we're talking about logic. We're really talking about our memories.

A Tale of Two Neighbors

Let me tell you about two neighbors I once knew.

Both lived on the same street. Both earned similar incomes. Both were, on paper, "middle class."

Neighbor One drove a five-year-old sedan. He and his wife packed lunches for work, took modest vacations, and quietly invested every month. If you saw him at the grocery store, you'd never know he was a millionaire.

Neighbor Two drove a luxury SUV. He remodeled his kitchen, wore expensive watches, and always had the latest phone. To everyone around, he looked successful.

Ten years later, Neighbor One had quietly built financial independence. He could choose whether to work. Neighbor Two was stressed, living paycheck to paycheck, with credit card debt hidden behind the granite countertops.

The difference wasn't knowledge. It was behavior.

Why We Misbehave with Money

You already know, deep down, what the smart things to do with money are. Spend less than you earn. Save consistently. Invest for the long term. Don't try to get rich overnight. Avoid debt that grows faster than your income.

And yet, if knowing and doing were the same thing, we wouldn't need books like this.

The challenge is not knowing what to do. The challenge is doing it when it feels uncomfortable.

When the market is down 40%.

When your neighbor just got rich on a coin you've never heard of.

When your boss drives up in a new car and you start to wonder if you're falling behind.

In those moments, knowledge takes a back seat. Psychology takes the wheel.

The Silent Teacher

When I was a kid, I watched my grandfather collect coins in glass jars.

He wasn't wealthy. He had a small pension and a simple life. But those jars represented security to him.

He had grown up in a time when banks failed and jobs vanished overnight. The lesson he learned—and passed down—was simple: **don't trust the future to be predictable.**

Decades later, I realized something: those jars weren't about interest rates or investment returns. They were about control. About feeling safe.

Today, we might laugh at the idea of saving coins in a jar instead of investing in an index fund. But for him, that jar was the most rational decision in the world, because it fit his psychology.

That's the thing: money decisions are rarely about being "right" in a universal sense. They are about being **right for you**.

The Cultural Illusion

Here's another story.

During the 2008 financial crisis, I met a couple who had built their entire identity around their dream home. They stretched to buy it. They furnished it with designer everything. And then—when the economy collapsed—they lost it all.

What hurt them the most wasn't losing the house. It was losing the identity they had wrapped around that house.

When money becomes a way to signal to the world who we are, it starts to control us instead of serve us.

Money Is a Mirror

Money doesn't change who we are. It just makes us more of what we already are.

If you're generous, more money makes you more generous. If you're insecure, more money makes you more insecure. If you're disciplined, money amplifies that discipline.

That's why you can't separate money from psychology. The two are glued together.

This Book Is Not About Becoming Rich

This is not a book about how to get rich. It's a book about how to think about money.

It's about how to recognize the hidden forces that drive financial behavior:

- *Luck and risk.*
- *Greed and fear.*

- *Patience and compounding.*
- *Comparison and contentment.*

It's about how to avoid the traps that cause smart people to make dumb money decisions. And it's about how to build a system for yourself that works with your psychology, not against it.

What You Can Expect

This book is built around stories. Some of these stories are about famous investors and companies; others are about ordinary people who made extraordinary (or disastrous) choices with money.

Each chapter ends with a short reflection—a few questions you can ask yourself. These aren't homework. They're pause buttons. They give you a chance to stop and think about what this all means for you.

You'll also see a few simple charts and tables. I promise these won't feel like a textbook. They're there to show patterns and make things easier to see.

Why You Might See Yourself in These Pages

You might find yourself nodding in recognition as you read. You might also find yourself squirming a bit. Both are good signs.

When you read about someone else's bad decision, it's easy to say, "I would never do that." But when you look closer, you realize you've done something similar—just in a different context.

The good news? Awareness is the first step toward change.

A Quick Reflection Before We Begin

Take a moment and think about these three questions:

1. *What is your first memory of money?*
2. *Who taught you—directly or indirectly—what money means?*
3. *What scares you more: losing money or missing out on an opportunity?*

Write your answers down. They will come back to you as we go through this book.

Because more than any chart or strategy, those answers explain why you behave the way you do.

The Goal

My goal isn't to make you smarter with numbers. My goal is to help you behave better with money.

Because behavior—patience, discipline, humility—is what separates those who build lasting wealth from those who lose it.

If you can master your behavior, you can make mistakes and still end up okay.
If you can't master your behavior, even a genius IQ won't save you.

So, let's begin with a simple truth:

Money isn't just a financial tool. It's a mirror. And what you see in that mirror has everything to do with you.

CHAPTER 1 - No One's Crazy

Money is one of the few things in life where two people can look at the same situation and come away with completely opposite reactions—and both be right.

Imagine a young man in 1979 who saw his father lose his job during an economic recession. That memory sits in his bones. Forty years later, he saves aggressively, keeps cash under the mattress, and avoids the stock market entirely. People might call him too conservative.

Now imagine a woman born in 1998. By the time she was old enough to notice, the economy had recovered from the financial crisis. She watched people become millionaires from startups, cryptocurrencies, and TikTok stardom. To her, risk-taking looks like a natural part of life. She invests almost everything she earns into high-growth companies. People might call her reckless.

Both are behaving rationally—**for their experience.**

The Lens of Experience

What we've lived through shapes how we see money.

If you were a teenager during a stock market crash, that memory stays with you like a scar. If you only experienced boom times, risk looks like opportunity.

The trouble is, we tend to assume that everyone sees the world as we do. They don't.

Our beliefs about money are not created in spreadsheets. They are carved into us by **what we've seen and what we've survived**.

The Great Divide

A study once asked people from different age groups where they preferred to keep their money.

- People who had lived through the Great Depression overwhelmingly said "cash and bonds."
- Younger investors preferred "stocks and real estate."

Same economy. Same country. Different answers.

Why? Because we don't make decisions from a spreadsheet. We make them from a story—**our own story.**

Case Study: Two Brothers, Two Paths

Meet Daniel and Chris.

- **Daniel** graduated college in 2009, right into the teeth of the financial crisis. It took him years to find a stable job. Even now, he never fully trusts the market. He saves in cash and owns very little stock.
- **Chris**, his younger brother, graduated in 2017. By then, the economy was booming. Chris invests everything he can into tech stocks and crypto.

At Thanksgiving dinner, they argue. Chris thinks Daniel is "leaving money on the table." Daniel thinks Chris is "gambling."

The truth? They are both behaving rationally, given what life has shown them.

The Illusion of Rationality

It's tempting to believe there's one "correct" way to behave with money. But rationality isn't a fixed standard. It's context.

- *To someone who's never lost a job, taking big risks feels rational.*
- *To someone who's been through layoffs, caution feels rational.*

And here's the key: **both of these approaches can work.**

Your Financial World Is Not Mine

Think about how personal finance advice is usually given:

- *"You should invest aggressively!"*
- *"Never carry debt!"*
- *"Always buy, never rent!"*

But here's the thing: advice is only good if it matches your life.

What works for a 22-year-old with no dependents and a stable job might be terrible advice for a 55-year-old who just got laid off and is paying for college tuition.

You can't copy someone else's financial strategy without copying their entire life. And you can't do that, because you're not them.

The Role of Scarcity and Abundance

Psychologists have found that people who grow up in scarcity often carry that mindset with them even after they become wealthy. This is why you'll meet rich people who still clip coupons. It's not that they need to—it's that their brains are wired to be cautious.

On the other side, people who grow up in abundance often underestimate risk. They assume the safety net will always be there because it always has been.

Neither group is wrong. They are just responding to what life has taught them.

Case Study: 2008 vs. 2021

In 2008, the global economy fell apart. People lost homes, jobs, and retirement savings. Those who lived through it became deeply cautious.

Fast forward to 2021. Interest rates were near zero, technology stocks were soaring, and millions of young investors opened trading accounts for the first time. To them, investing wasn't scary; it was a game.

If you ask someone who started investing in 2008 what they think of 2021 behavior, they might call it crazy. But if you ask someone who started in 2021, they might call 2008-era caution "old-fashioned."

Same world. Different worlds.

The Mirage of "Right" and "Wrong"

The next time you see someone make a financial decision you don't understand, try this:
Instead of saying, "That's crazy," ask, "What do they know that I don't?"

They may have a scar you can't see. They may have a fear you've never felt. They may have an opportunity you don't have.

Money Is Emotional Before It Is Logical

One of the most important realizations about money is that **people don't want the highest returns—they want the returns they can live with.**

- The investor who sells during every downturn isn't dumb; they just value sleep more than squeezing out an extra 1%.

- The person who pays off a mortgage early, even when interest rates are low, isn't ignorant; they just value peace of mind over math.

These are emotional decisions, yes. But they are also **valid decisions**, because they fit the person making them.

Case Study: Two Retirees

Take two retirees, Susan and Mark.

- **Susan** keeps a large portion of her savings in bonds, even when stocks are soaring. Her kids tell her she could make more in the market. But Susan remembers being 10 years old, sitting at the kitchen table while her parents argued about losing their house. For her, safety is worth more than growth.
- **Mark**, on the other hand, invests heavily in stocks. He knows the market can be bumpy, but he grew up

in a family that never lost much during recessions. To him, volatility feels like a normal part of life.

Who is right?

Both of them.

The Takeaway

There is no single rational way to handle money.

There are only decisions that are rational for you, based on your personality, experiences, and goals.

When you understand this, a lot of financial conflict disappears. You stop seeing others as crazy, and you start seeing them as different.

Think About This

Before moving on, pause for a moment and reflect on these questions:

1. What's the most vivid money-related experience from your childhood?
2. How does that experience still influence your decisions today?
3. Do you ever assume others think about money the way you do?

Write your answers in a notebook or on your phone. This little exercise will help you get more out of every chapter that follows.

Closing Thought

The world is full of different kinds of financial behavior. Some of it looks reckless. Some of it looks overly cautious. But when you look closer, almost none of it is crazy.

It's just people making choices that make sense to them—based on the world as they've experienced it.

And that's where we'll begin our journey.

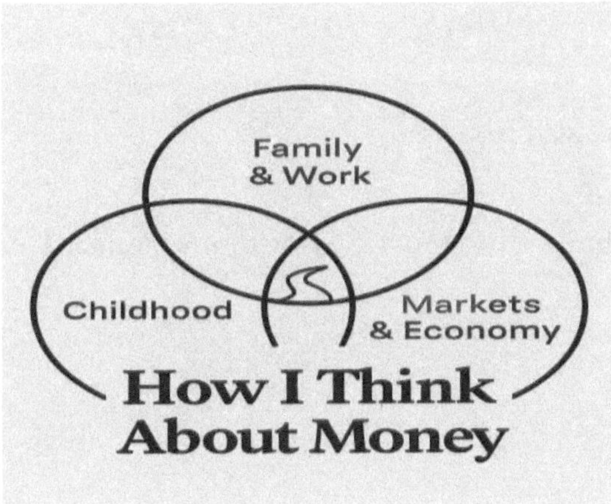

Table 1 – How Life Events Shape Money Behavior

Life Experience	Typical Behavior Pattern
Grew up during a recession	High savings rate, cautious investing
Grew up during an economic boom	Risk-tolerant, more aggressive investing
Experienced sudden job loss	Prefers stability and emergency funds
Watched peers get rich quickly	More willing to speculate or take risks

Reflection Exercise

Think About This:

1. What's the most vivid money-related experience from your childhood?
2. How does that experience still influence your decisions today?
3. Do you assume others think about money the way you do?

Take 10 minutes to jot down your answers before moving forward.

CHAPTER 2 - Luck & Risk

The Two Sides of Every Story

We love to believe success is the result of hard work. We also like to believe failure is the result of bad decisions.

But when it comes to money, neither story is ever that simple.

There is **always** an invisible partner at play: luck and risk.

Luck is the wind at your back that you didn't create. Risk is the storm you didn't see coming.

Understanding this difference is one of the most humbling lessons in finance.

Bill Gates and the Computer Lab

In 1968, a teenage Bill Gates walked into one of the only high schools in the world with a computer terminal. That single stroke of luck gave him access to technology most college students didn't have.

Did he work incredibly hard? Absolutely. Did he take risks? Without question.

But without that computer lab, there might not have been a Microsoft.

That's luck.

Luck Is Not an Excuse, but It Is Real

This doesn't mean Gates didn't earn his success. It means **success is rarely 100% earned**. And failure is rarely 100% deserved.

We live in a world that loves simple stories. "He's rich because he's brilliant."

"She failed because she made mistakes."

The truth is more complex. Life is messy. Outcomes are influenced by dozens of factors you can't control.

Why This Matters

The danger of ignoring luck and risk is twofold:

1. **You overestimate your own skill.** You think every good outcome is the result of brilliance.
2. **You underestimate other people's struggles.** You think every failure is due to stupidity.

Both lead to arrogance.

We love to believe success is the result of hard work. We also like to believe failure is the result of bad decisions.

But when it comes to money, neither story is ever that simple.

There is **always** an invisible partner at play: luck and risk.

Luck is the wind at your back that you didn't create. Risk is the storm you didn't see coming.

Understanding this difference is one of the most humbling lessons in finance.

Bill Gates and the Computer Lab

In 1968, a teenage Bill Gates walked into one of the only high schools in the world with a computer terminal. That single stroke of luck gave him access to technology most college students didn't have.

Did he work incredibly hard? Absolutely. Did he take risks? Without question.

But without that computer lab, there might not have been a Microsoft.

That's luck.

The Hidden Role of Luck

This doesn't mean Gates didn't earn his success. It means **success is rarely 100% earned**. And failure is rarely 100% deserved.

We live in a world that loves simple stories.

- "He's rich because he's brilliant."
- "She failed because she made mistakes."

The truth is more complex. Life is messy. Outcomes are influenced by dozens of factors you can't control.

Case Study: The Tech Boom Lottery

In the late 1990s, a few young programmers in Silicon Valley created startups that changed the world. Some became billionaires. Others, with similar talent and ideas, worked just as hard but joined companies that went bankrupt during the dot-com crash.

The difference? Timing. Market conditions. Luck.

You can be brilliant, disciplined, and hardworking—and still end up with nothing because the wave you tried to ride collapsed under you.

And Then, There's Risk

If luck is a tailwind you didn't earn, risk is a pothole you didn't see.

- The entrepreneur who launches a great business—right before a global pandemic.
- The investor who follows a sound plan—right before a financial crisis.
- The diligent saver whose medical bills wipe out years of planning.

None of these outcomes are "fair." That's because life isn't fair.

Russian Roulette

Here's a thought experiment:

Suppose you play a game of Russian roulette with one bullet in a six-chamber revolver. You pull the trigger, and nothing happens.

Are you smart or lucky?

The answer is obvious: lucky.

But in finance, when someone takes wild risks and comes out ahead, we tend to call them a genius. We confuse survival with skill.

The flip side is true as well: when someone makes a prudent decision that ends badly, we call them a fool. We confuse bad luck with bad judgment.

Learning the Right Lessons

The danger in mixing up luck and risk is that you learn the wrong lessons.

- If you succeed purely due to luck, you may think you're invincible and double down on reckless behavior.
- If you fail purely due to risk, you may stop trying altogether, even if your process was sound.

What matters is **distinguishing the process from the outcome**.

Case Study: Warren Buffett and Long-Term Thinking

Warren Buffett is famous for saying that his skill is choosing where to be lucky. He can't control market crashes or random events, but he builds his investing philosophy to maximize the role of time and minimize the role of bad luck.

He invests in a way that doesn't require perfection.

He leaves room for mistakes.

And he never lets short-term outcomes fool him into thinking he's a genius—or an idiot.

The Ego Trap

We love to take credit when things go well and blame bad luck when they don't.

This is human nature.

- When you make a great investment, you think, *I'm so smart.*
- When it fails, you think, *the market is rigged against me.*

But the truth is: both success and failure are a mix of **skill, effort, and factors outside your control.**

What This Means for You

Understanding the roles of luck and risk leads to two crucial insights:

1. **Be humble in success.**
    - Realize that not all of it was your doing.
    - Share credit with timing and circumstances.
2. **Be forgiving in failure.**
    - Don't let one bad outcome define you.
    - Sometimes, you did everything right—and the world still went wrong.

The Illusion of Total Control

There is a dangerous belief that if you just learn enough, plan enough, and work hard enough, you can control everything.

You can't.

Even the most meticulous plans can be undone by one unpredictable event.

The goal isn't control. It's **resilience.**

How to Apply This Lesson

- **Focus on your process, not your outcome.**

  Judge your decisions based on the information you had at the time, not the result that happened afterward.

- **Leave room for randomness.**

  Build margin into your finances. Assume surprises will happen.

- **Stay humble.**

  If you succeed, say, *I did well, and I was fortunate.* If you fail, say, *I did my best, and I learned something.*

Case Study: The 2020 Pandemic

No one saw it coming. Even the most prepared investors and business owners faced enormous challenges.

- Airlines with decades of profits nearly went bankrupt.
- Small businesses with loyal customers shut their doors.
- Millions of people who did everything “right” financially had to start over.

This is why **arrogance is dangerous**: the belief that you're immune to surprises is the surest way to be humbled by them.

A Different Way to Think About Risk

Risk isn't just about losing money.

Risk is **everything that can go wrong that you haven't thought of yet**.

The market can crash. Your health can change. The rules of the game can shift. Entire industries can disappear.

Which is why the best financial plan is not the one with the highest return.

It's the one that **can survive the most surprises.**

Reflection: What's in Your Control?

Here's what you can control:

- How much you save
- How much you spend
- How much risk you choose to take
- How patient you are
- How you react when things don't go as planned

Here's what you **can't** control:

- The timing of recessions
- Inflation
- Interest rates
- Stock market crashes
- Sudden life events

Focus on what's in your hands. Build a margin for everything else.

Think About This

Before moving on, ask yourself:

1. Have I ever mistaken good luck for skill?
2. When something went wrong in my life, did I blame myself for things I couldn't control?
3. How can I build more margin into my finances so that unexpected events don't destroy me?

Write these down. They will shape how you view risk for the rest of this book.

Closing Thought

Here's the paradox:

- Luck and risk are invisible until after they've already happened.

- Yet they are the single biggest forces shaping your financial life.

The best you can do is respect their power, stay humble, and never let success or failure go to your head.

Table 2 – Factors Outside Your Control

Factor	Possible Impact
Timing of birth	What economy you grow up in
Market cycles	When you start investing
Random events	Health, pandemics, layoffs

CHAPTER 3 - Never Enough

There's a story about a famous hedge fund manager who was once asked why he kept taking bigger and bigger risks even after he was already worth hundreds of millions.

His answer?

"Because someone else has a billion."

A year later, he lost almost everything.

The Moving Goalpost

One of the most dangerous ideas in money—and in life—is that success means **more**.

- More money.
- A bigger house.
- A newer car.
- A promotion.

- Another zero on your net worth.

The problem with "more" is that there is no finish line.

If your definition of success is always moving, you will never arrive.

When Enough Isn't Enough

At some point, the pursuit of wealth stops being about comfort and starts being about competition. You're no longer trying to live better—you're trying to live better **than someone else**.

And that game has no winner.

Case Study: Rajat Gupta

Rajat Gupta grew up poor in India, rose to become the CEO of McKinsey & Company, and had a net worth of over $100 million. He had power, respect, and access to opportunities most people could only dream of.

But he wanted more.

He was convicted of insider trading after trying to make even more money through illegal tips.

Why? Because being rich wasn't enough. He wanted to be **richer**.

Comparison Is a Thief

When we compare ourselves to others, we set ourselves up for misery.

There will always be someone with:

- A nicer car

- A bigger house
- A better job
- More followers

The irony is that many of those people are also comparing themselves to someone else.

It's a race with no finish line.

What Does Enough Look Like?

Most people never stop to define what "enough" means to them. So, they chase it forever.

- Is it a specific amount of money?
- Is it a certain lifestyle?
- Is it the ability to say "no" to things you don't want to do?

If you don't know, the chase will never stop.

The Quiet Millionaire

I once met a man in his 60s who retired early with a modest home and a simple lifestyle. By most modern standards, he didn't "look" wealthy.

When I asked him if he ever wished he had more, he smiled and said, "Why would I trade what I already have for stress I don't need? I have enough."

That sentence stayed with me.

Because "enough" is a superpower.

When More Becomes Dangerous

There's a point where chasing more becomes riskier than standing still.

- You over-leverage yourself trying to make a quick fortune.

- You spend everything you earn to keep up appearances.
- You gamble on investments because steady growth feels too slow.

All because you think **"just a little more"** will finally make you happy.

Case Study: Long-Term Capital Management

In the 1990s, Long-Term Capital Management was run by some of the smartest financial minds in the world—including two Nobel Prize winners.

They made incredible returns. Then they decided to push for more. They used massive leverage, betting that markets would stay stable.

They were wrong.

In 1998, they lost billions almost overnight, and the U.S. government had to step in to prevent a financial collapse.

If they had stopped a year earlier, they would have been legends. Instead, they became a cautionary tale.

Enough Is Relative

Here's the thing: there's no universal definition of "enough."

- For some, enough is $50,000 a year and a quiet life.
- For others, enough is $500,000 a year and travel around the world.

Neither is right or wrong.

The key is that **you** decide, not society.

Why Enough Is So Hard

There are two big reasons we struggle to feel like we have enough:

1. **Social Comparison**

   We compare ourselves upward, not downward. We notice people who have more, not those who have less.

2. **Adaptation**

   Humans adapt quickly. The thing that once felt luxurious soon becomes normal. So we need more to feel the same satisfaction.

This is called the **hedonic treadmill**—and if you're not careful, you can run on it forever.

The Antidote: Gratitude

The simplest way to feel like you have enough is to regularly remind yourself of what you already have.

Take a moment to list three things you have today that you once wished for. It could be:

- A stable job
- A safe home
- Good health
- Friends you trust

Those things are easy to forget. But they are wealth.

The Real Reward of Enough

When you have enough, you gain:

- Peace of mind

- The ability to say "no"
- Freedom to focus on what matters

Ironically, this is what most people are chasing when they chase money. They just don't realize that more money won't necessarily bring it.

Building Your Own Definition of Enough

Here are three steps to define your own version:

1. **Set Your Finish Line**

   Decide what you need to feel secure and content. Write it down.

2. **Practice Contentment**

   Regularly check in with yourself. Are you chasing more out of need—or out of comparison?

3. **Protect It**

   Don't risk what you have for what you don't need.

Reflection Prompt: What Would Make You Say "I Have Enough"?

Close your eyes and imagine that today is ten years from now.

- How much money do you need in the bank to feel secure?
- What does your daily life look like?
- Who are you trying to impress? (If the answer is "no one," you're already ahead.)

Think About This

Before moving on, ask yourself:

1. What is "enough" for me? Have I written it down?
2. Have I ever risked something I needed for something I didn't?

3. Who am I comparing myself to, and why?

Closing Thought

Wealth is not just about having more.

It's about knowing when to stop.

People who understand "enough" may not always look like the richest, but they often live the richest lives.

Table 3 – Enough vs. Never Enough:

Mindset	**Result**
Enough	Peace, stability, focus
Never Enough	Stress, greed, burnout

CHAPTER 4 - The Power of Compounding

Albert Einstein reportedly called compounding the "eighth wonder of the world." Whether he actually said that doesn't matter—the idea itself is true.

Compounding is simple: **small gains, repeated consistently, grow into something extraordinary.**

But here's the catch: because it looks boring in the short run, most people underestimate it in the long run.

The Magic Nobody Notices

Imagine planting a seed.

For weeks, you water it and…nothing.

Months pass. Still, nothing impressive.

Then, seemingly overnight, it sprouts. And in a few years, it becomes a tree.

That's how compounding works.

It's invisible until suddenly, it isn't.

Case Study: Warren Buffett's Fortune

People often say Warren Buffett is a financial genius—and he is. But his real secret isn't picking stocks. It's **time**.

- *Buffett started investing at age 10.*
- *By the time he was 30, he was already a millionaire.*
- *Today, over 90% of his wealth came after he turned 60.*

If Buffett had started investing in his 30s instead of his 10s, his net worth would be a fraction of what it is today. His greatest investment skill is patience.

Why Compounding Works

Compounding works because **your returns also earn returns**. The cycle feeds on itself.

- If you invest $1 and earn 10%, you now have $1.10.
- Next year, you earn 10% on $1.10—not just $1.
- That extra 10 cents also earns 10% in the next round.

This simple loop creates exponential growth.

The Graph That Explains Everything

If you draw a chart of compounding growth, it looks flat for a long time, then curves sharply upward.

Flat. Flat. Flat. Boom.

The early years feel slow. Then, suddenly, the numbers take off. That final curve is where the magic happens.

Why Most People Quit Too Soon

Here's the problem:

Most people get bored or discouraged during the "flat" part of compounding. They want fast results. When they don't see them, they change strategies, withdraw their money, or chase something that looks more exciting.

But the people who win are the ones who **stay in the game long enough for the curve to appear.**

Case Study: The Marathon Saver

I once met a woman named Hannah who started saving just $100 a month when she was 25. She didn't increase it for years. She just kept going, through recessions and market crashes.

At 55, she had far more money than her friends who made larger contributions but kept jumping in and out of the market trying to “time” it.

Her edge wasn’t size. It was **consistency.**

The Time Factor

There are two parts to compounding:

1. **Rate of return** (how much you earn)
2. **Time** (how long you stay invested)

Time matters more than rate.

Why? Because missing out on compounding time can’t be made up by higher returns later.

Example: Start Early vs. Start Late

- **Person A:** Starts investing $200/month at age 25, stops at 35, and never invests again.

- **Person B:** Waits until 35, then invests $200/month all the way until 65.

Who has more money at 65?

Person A.

Even though Person B invested three times more money, Person A had a ten-year head start. Time beats effort.

The Human Bias Against Slow Growth

We are wired for instant gratification. Fast results feel exciting. Slow results feel like failure.

But compounding is a **slow burn.**

- It's like boiling water. Nothing happens for a while. Then suddenly, steam.
- It's like watching grass grow. Boring…until one day, it's a field.

The patience it requires is rare—and that's why it works.

Case Study: Amazon's Early Years

If you bought Amazon stock in 1997 and held on, you'd have seen 95% drops in its value more than once. Most people sold during those drops.

The few who stayed? They became millionaires.

The market rewarded **time in** over **timing**.

Not Just About Money

Compounding isn't just a financial concept. It applies to:

- Knowledge
- Habits
- Relationships
- Health

The small choices you make every day—good or bad—compound over decades into something massive.

Practical Ways to Harness Compounding

1. **Start Early**

   Even small amounts matter. Time multiplies them.

2. **Be Consistent**

   Automate savings and investments. Let them grow in the background.

3. **Stay Patient**

   Ignore short-term ups and downs. Think in decades.

4. **Avoid Interrupting the Cycle**

   Don't constantly switch strategies or pull-out money.

Reflection Prompt: The 10-Year Rule

Ask yourself:

If I made this decision and didn't see any results for 10 years, would I still do it?

If the answer is yes, you're likely building something that will compound.

Think About This

1. Where in your life are you quitting too early?
2. Are you focused on quick wins or long-term gains?
3. How can you build more patience into your financial plan?

Closing Thought

The most powerful force in finance isn't intelligence, luck, or timing.

It's patience.

When you give your money—and your decisions—time, small actions grow into extraordinary results.

Table 4 – Small Consistent Effort vs. Sporadic Big Effort

Approach	Result After 30 Years
$200/month, consistent	Large nest egg
Sporadic lump sums	Smaller balance (due to missed time)

CHAPTER 5 - Getting Wealthy vs. Staying Wealthy

There is a big difference between **getting rich** and **staying rich**.

Getting wealthy requires one set of skills: courage, risk-taking, hard work, optimism.
Staying wealthy requires an almost opposite set: humility, restraint, and fear.

Most people are good at one. Few are good at both.

Part I – The Two Different Games

Imagine a mountain climber.
The skills that get them to the summit—strength, speed, and boldness—are not the same skills that will get them back down safely.

In fact, most mountaineering accidents happen **on the way down**, not on the way up.

Wealth works the same way.

- Getting to the top is one game.
- Staying there is another.

The Upward Climb: Getting Wealthy

To build wealth, you need:

- **Risk-taking:** Starting a business, investing, believing you can succeed.
- **Optimism:** The confidence that your efforts will pay off.
- **Ambition:** A hunger to push beyond comfort zones.

You don't grow wealth by being timid. You have to take shots.

The Descent: Staying Wealthy

But once you've climbed, the rules change.

To keep wealth, you need:

- **Humility:** Knowing that success doesn't make you invincible.
- **Frugality:** Spending less than you could.
- **Risk Awareness:** Avoiding decisions that could wipe everything out.

Where the first game requires taking chances, the second game is about **protecting what you've already earned**.

Part II – Why People Lose Wealth

The most common way people lose wealth isn't a bad market. It's a **bad mindset.**

Here are three patterns that show up again and again:

1. Overconfidence

Success makes us believe we're smarter than we are. We forget that some part of our success came from luck or timing. We start to think we can't lose.

- The investor who gets rich on a few stock picks decides to use leverage and loses it all.
- The business owner who thrives in one decade expands too fast and collapses in the next.

Arrogance after success is the single biggest wealth destroyer.

2. No Margin for Error

When everything you have is tied up in risky bets, you leave no room for surprises.

- If you build wealth by risking everything, you can lose it the same way.

- Staying wealthy means **building a buffer**, even if it slows you down.

3. Forgetting What Got You There

Many people assume that the behavior that helped them grow their wealth will also help them keep it. But the skills that got you **to** the top aren't the same skills that keep you **on** the top.

Case Study: The Dot-Com Era

In the late 1990s, tech investors made fortunes as internet companies soared. Many assumed the boom would last forever. They doubled down, using leverage to make even bigger bets.

Then, the bubble burst. By 2002, many of those paper millionaires were bankrupt.

The lesson: **Getting rich made them fearless. Staying rich required fear.**

Part III – The Mindset Shift

The best investors I know have two personalities:

- **Bold when building.**
- **Cautious when protecting.**

It's a paradox. You need to know when to switch gears.

"I Might Be Wrong"

The investors who last the longest share a simple mantra: **"I might be wrong."**

- They diversify because they know they don't know everything.

- They hold cash because they know markets can surprise them.
- They live below their means because they know good times don't last forever.

This humility keeps them in the game long after others have fallen out.

Survivorship Bias

It's tempting to look at someone who has been rich for decades and assume they're just smarter. But the truth is that **long-term wealth is often more about survival than brilliance**.

The ones who last aren't those who took the biggest risks—they're the ones who avoided the fatal ones.

Part IV – How to Stay Wealthy

1. Build a Margin of Safety

Always keep enough cash or safe assets to survive bad markets, job losses, or unexpected expenses.

2. Respect Volatility

Assume downturns are coming. Plan for them in advance.

3. Stay Humble

Past success doesn't guarantee future safety. Approach every new decision as if you could be wrong.

4. Protect Your Downside

Don't let a single bad bet ruin your life. Spread your risks.

5. Define "Enough"

If you never decide what's enough, you'll always take more risk than you should.

Case Study: A Tale of Two Investors

- **Investor A:** Doubled his portfolio in five years by taking risky bets. Then he kept taking risks, refused to diversify, and lost everything in one market downturn.
- **Investor B:** Grew slower, diversified, stayed cautious, and ended up with a smaller gain early—but decades later, she had far more wealth because she survived.

The difference?

Survival beats speed.

Part V – The Quiet Formula

Here's a simple formula for long-term wealth:

Wealth = (Getting Rich × Staying Rich)

- If you only know how to grow but not protect, you end up back at zero.
- If you only know how to protect but never grow, you never build anything significant.
- You need both.

Case Study: Warren Buffett (Again)

Buffett is a perfect example.

He built wealth through optimism and long-term investing—but he **protects** that wealth by holding cash, diversifying, and avoiding unnecessary risks.

It's why he has stayed relevant for seven decades.

A Quote Worth Remembering

Financial advisor Nick Murray once said:

"The goal is not to get rich fast. The goal is to stay rich for a lifetime."

The Emotional Challenge

Staying wealthy is emotionally harder than getting wealthy because it requires you to go against your own instincts.

- When things are going well, you have to **fight greed**.
- When things are going badly, you have to **fight fear**.

Discipline in both directions is rare—and valuable.

Practical Reflection: What Would Ruin You?

Take out a piece of paper and write down:

- What single event could wipe out everything you've built?
- How can you protect against that event?

This exercise might feel uncomfortable. That's good. The more you prepare for bad outcomes, the less damage they do when they arrive.

Think About This

Before moving on, reflect:

1. Am I better at building wealth or keeping it?
2. What's my plan to survive a worst-case scenario?
3. Have I confused success with invincibility?

Closing Thought

Getting wealthy is about offense.

Staying wealthy is about defense.

If you want to win the game of money, you have to play both halves.

Otherwise, history will treat you like the climber who reached the summit and didn't make it back down.

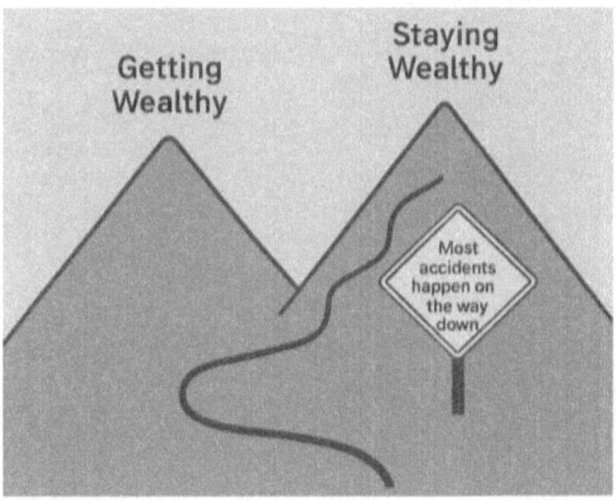

Two Mountains

- First peak: "Getting Wealthy"

- Second peak: "Staying Wealthy"

  A path connecting them, with a warning sign: *Most accidents happen on the way down.*

Table 5 – Skills for Each Stage

Stage	**Key Skills**
Getting Wealthy	Risk-taking, optimism, ambition
Staying Wealthy	Humility, frugality, caution

CHAPTER 6 - Tails, You Win

In investing and in life, **most things don't matter.**

That sounds strange, but it's true. A tiny number of events—what statisticians call "long tails"—are responsible for the majority of outcomes.

The 80/20 Rule on Steroids

You may have heard of the 80/20 rule: 80% of results come from 20% of actions.

In finance, the ratio is even more extreme. It might be 90/10, or even 99/1.

- A few stocks drive most of the stock market's gains.
- A few key decisions shape the trajectory of a business.
- A few unexpected events change the world.

Most of the time, not much happens. And then, once in a while, **everything happens at once.**

Case Study: Venture Capital

Venture capital firms know this better than anyone. They invest in dozens of startups expecting that:

- *Most will fail.*
- *A few will break even.*
- *One or two will make so much money that it pays for all the losses.*

That's a tail.

Facebook, Uber, Airbnb—these weren't just good investments. They were **tail events** that produced massive results.

Apple and the iPhone

Before 2007, Apple was a successful company. After the iPhone launched, Apple became one of the most valuable companies in history.

One product—a single tail event—changed everything.

The Role of Luck and Tail Events

This connects back to Chapter 2.

Tail events are partly skill and partly luck. You can't predict exactly when they'll happen. You just have to **be around long enough to catch one.**

Why This Matters for Investors

- You don't need to be right all the time.
- You just need to be **right big once in a while—and survive long enough to experience it.**

This is why staying invested, even through downturns, is so critical. If you miss the handful of best market days in a decade, you miss most of the gains.

How Tails Show Up in Life

Tails aren't just in finance:

- **Career:** One key relationship can change your career.
- **Health:** One habit can dramatically improve your health.
- **Relationships:** One person can change your entire social circle.

Not all days are created equal. **A small number of days matter more than the rest combined.**

The Patience Problem

The challenge with tails is that **they require patience.**

You might go through years where nothing big happens. You feel stuck, bored, maybe even foolish for sticking to your plan. And then one event suddenly makes it all worth it.

- An investor sits through ten flat years, then one market boom triples their wealth.
- An entrepreneur fails five times, then one idea takes off and pays for everything.

Case Study: Jeff Bezos and Amazon

Jeff Bezos once said that Amazon has made "billions of dollars of failures." They've launched countless products that didn't work out.

But AWS, Prime, and the Kindle? Those three "tails" more than covered every failure.

Most Things Don't Matter

One of the best ways to build wealth is to **focus on surviving the boring stretches** so you're still around when a tail event comes.

The mistake most people make is giving up too soon. They quit because the early years are slow, or because they're chasing quick wins.

Investing Example: Missing the Big Days

If you look at the last 30 years of the U.S. stock market, almost all of the gains came from a handful of days:

- The 10 best days accounted for the majority of returns.
- If you missed those days, your returns were dramatically lower.

Those days are impossible to predict. They often come right after the worst days.

So, the only way to catch them is to stay invested through both.

How to Prepare for Tails

1. **Expect them.**

   Understand that a small number of decisions will drive most results.

2. **Diversify.**

   Spread out your efforts so you can afford to be wrong many times.

3. **Stay in the game.**

   The longer you're around, the more likely you are to catch a tail event.

4. **Don't overreact to small losses.**

   Focus on the few things that matter most.

When Tails Go Negative

Just as there are positive tails, there are **negative tails**:

- One bad habit that wrecks your health.
- One bad decision that ruins a reputation.
- One catastrophic risk that wipes out wealth.

This is why **risk management is just as important as seeking opportunity.**

Case Study: A Negative Tail – The 2008 Crisis

The global financial crisis was a negative tail event.

- Years of seemingly safe mortgage lending suddenly turned toxic.

- Entire companies vanished in weeks.
- Families who thought they were secure lost everything.

One event undid years of growth.

You Need Only a Few Big Wins

There's a comforting lesson here: **You don't have to get everything right.**

- You don't have to start 100 successful companies—just one.
- You don't have to pick every winning stock—just a few.
- You don't have to be perfect every day—just avoid ruin and keep moving forward.

Reflection Prompt: Identify Your "Tails"

Think about:

- What are the **few key decisions** or events that could completely change your future?
- Are you in a position to recognize them—and take advantage of them—when they appear?

Think About This

1. What tail events—positive or negative—have shaped your life so far?
2. Am I too focused on being right all the time, instead of being patient?
3. How can I make sure I'm still standing when the next big opportunity comes?

Closing Thought

Life is not a straight line.

It's long stretches of small, boring steps—punctuated by a few events that change everything.

If you want to win, you don't need to be right all the time. You just need to **stay in the game long enough for the tails to show up—and not blow yourself up before they do.**

Table 6 – How Tails Work

Number of Events	Contribution to Outcome
90% of events	Little to no impact
10% of events	Most of the impact

CHAPTER 7 - Freedom

If you ask most people what they want from money, they'll tell you things like:

- A bigger house
- A nicer car
- Luxury vacations

But if you dig deeper, what they really want isn't the stuff. It's **freedom**.

Freedom to do what they want, when they want, with whom they want.

Freedom is the **ultimate dividend of wealth.**

Part I – Time: The Real Currency

Time is the one thing you can't make more of. No matter how much money you have, you get the same 24 hours in a day as everyone else.

So the ultimate purpose of money is not just to buy things—it's to **buy time**.

Case Study: The Unhappy Millionaire

I once met a man worth $20 million. He had the house, the cars, the vacation homes.

But he was miserable. Why?

Because his wealth came with obligations:

- A business that consumed every waking hour
- Endless calls, meetings, and decisions
- No time for his family

He had money, but **he didn't own his time**.

The Happy Teacher

Contrast that with a schoolteacher I know who never earned more than $60,000 a year. She lives modestly, but she has:

- Summers off
- Time to spend with her kids
- Weekends free from stress

She feels wealthy—not because of a big bank account, but because **she owns her days**.

The Trap of "More"

Money without freedom is like a golden cage. You have the means to do whatever you want—but no time to do it.

We often chase promotions, bonuses, and bigger salaries thinking they will bring happiness. But what they often bring is **less freedom**: more responsibility, more pressure, more commitments.

Part II – Why We Crave Autonomy

Psychologists have found that **autonomy**—the ability to control your own time—is one of the strongest predictors of happiness.

- When you feel forced to do something, it becomes stressful, even if you enjoy the activity.
- When you choose to do something, it feels fulfilling, even if it's hard work.

This is why retirees often say their favorite thing about retirement isn't the lack of work—it's the lack of **obligation**.

A Day without Freedom vs. A Day with Freedom

- **Without freedom:** Wake up to an alarm you hate. Rush to a job you can't stand. Spend your day doing tasks you didn't choose.
- **With freedom:** Wake up on your own time. Decide what matters today. Spend your time with people and projects you value.

Which sounds wealthier?

Part III – The Subtle Cost of Losing Control

When you don't own your time:

- Your health suffers (because stress steals your energy)
- Your relationships suffer (because you're never present)

- Your creativity dies (because you're always reacting)

Money can amplify these problems if you're not careful.

The wrong kind of wealth can trap you.

Case Study: The Executive Who Walked Away

I once interviewed an executive who quit a seven-figure job. People thought he was crazy. Why would you walk away from that kind of money?

His answer:

"I realized I was working 80 hours a week to afford things I didn't have time to enjoy."

Today, he earns less, but he has his life back.

Freedom Doesn't Require Millions

There's a misconception that freedom requires extraordinary wealth. It doesn't.

Often, freedom is a function of **spending less** rather than earning more.

- If your expenses are low, you don't need to work as hard.
- If you avoid debt, you avoid being trapped by it.
- If you define "enough," you can buy your time back sooner.

Mini-Retirements

Entrepreneur Tim Ferriss popularized the concept of **mini-retirements**: instead of waiting until 65 to enjoy life, take smaller breaks throughout your career.

This approach treats time as the most precious asset—and allocates it **while you're still young enough to enjoy it.**

Part IV – How to Buy Back Your Time

Here are three practical ways to use money to buy freedom:

1. Build an Emergency Fund

An emergency fund isn't just for financial security—it's for **psychological freedom**.

When you know you can survive a job loss or a surprise expense, you make decisions from a place of strength, not fear.

2. Pay Off Debt

Debt is a contract to trade your future time for money today. The fewer obligations you have, the more freedom you gain.

3. Live Below Your Means

Every dollar you don't spend on status is a dollar you can use to buy control of your life. Simple living often means more control.

The Power of "No"

Money without the ability to say "no" isn't real wealth.

The ability to say "no" to things that don't matter—to people, obligations, and work that drain you—is one of the greatest privileges money can buy.

Reflection Prompt: What Would You Do with One Free Day?

Close your eyes and imagine you have a full day with no obligations.

- What would you do?

- Who would you spend it with?
- What would you avoid?

The answers to these questions tell you what freedom means to you.

Part V – The Journey Toward Freedom

Step 1: Define What Matters

Freedom isn't about doing nothing. It's about doing what matters most to you.

For some, that means travel. For others, it's creative work, volunteering, or spending time with family.

Step 2: Design Your Finances Around That Goal

Every financial decision you make—how much you spend, how much you save, how you invest—should be guided by this question:

"Will this give me more control over my time?"

Step 3: Protect Your Time Like You Protect Your Money

Say "no" to things that don't align with your values. Guard your calendar as fiercely as your wallet.

Case Study: The Designer Who Downsized

A successful graphic designer I know deliberately cut her workload in half. She also downsized to a smaller apartment, sold her car, and stopped chasing luxury clients.

Her income dropped by 40%. Her happiness skyrocketed by 100%.

Her words:

"I finally feel like I own my life."

The Freedom Formula

Here's a simple framework:

Freedom = (Savings Rate × Low Expenses) + Control Over Time

You can achieve freedom in two ways:

- Increase your income without increasing your lifestyle, or
- Keep your lifestyle simple so you need less income.

The Paradox: Freedom Is the Real Flex

In a world obsessed with showing off wealth, the real status symbol is **control over your time**.

The ability to do what you want, when you want, without asking for permission—that's true luxury.

What Freedom Feels Like

- Waking up without an alarm
- Choosing who you work with
- Deciding when to take a break
- Saying “no” without guilt

These are small things. But they add up to a big life.

Think About This

1. What does freedom look like to me?
2. Am I making financial decisions that move me closer to—or further away from—owning my time?
3. If I had complete control over my time, what would I stop doing tomorrow?

Closing Thought

We chase money because we think it will make us happy. But money is just a tool. The real prize is **freedom**.

If you can buy back your time, you've already won. And the best part? You don't need millions to get there.

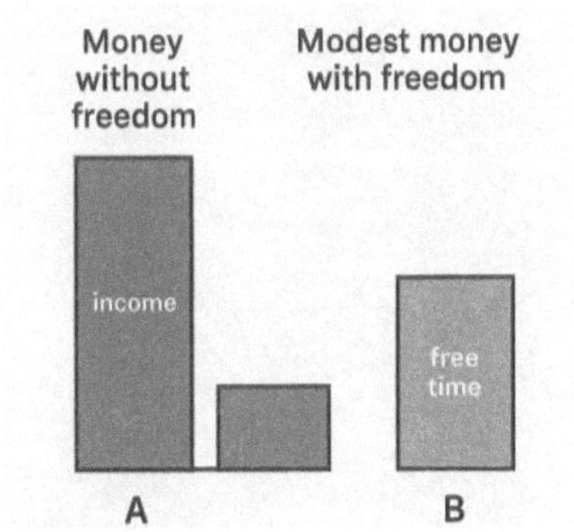

Visual 7 – Two Bars:

- Bar A: Money without freedom → Tall bar labeled "income" but small bar labeled "free time."
- Bar B: Modest money with freedom → Shorter income bar, but full, tall bar labeled "free time."

Table 7 – Freedom vs. Constraint

High Income, No Freedom	**Modest Income, High Freedom**
Busy schedule	Flexible schedule
Stressful work	Chosen work
No time to enjoy wealth	Plenty of time for life

CHAPTER 8 - The Man in the Car Paradox

There's a curious paradox about expensive things: The people you hope to impress by buying them usually **aren't thinking about you at all.**

Part I – Why We Buy Impressive Things

We all crave respect.

- We want people to admire us.
- We want to be seen as successful.
- We want to feel like we matter.

So, we often buy things that we think will signal success:

- A luxury car
- A big house
- Designer clothes
- A watch that costs as much as a used car

These things are symbols. They say: *Look at me! I made it.*

But here's the paradox: **people don't see you. They see the car.**

Case Study: The Red Convertible

Imagine a man driving a bright red sports car. Heads turn as he drives past.

What are people thinking?

- "Wow, that's a nice car."
- "I'd love to drive something like that."

What they are **not** thinking is:

- "Wow, I really admire the driver."

The admiration doesn't transfer to the person. It stays with the car.

The Respect We Think We're Buying

We assume that possessions will make people respect us. But most of the time, **people don't care about us nearly as much as we think.**

They're too busy thinking about themselves.

Psychological Insight: The Spotlight Effect

Behavioral psychologists call this the **spotlight effect**:

- We overestimate how much people notice us.
- In reality, most people barely notice what we're doing—they're thinking about their own lives.

That expensive purchase you made to impress people? Most of them won't even remember it tomorrow.

Part II – What Really Earns Respect

Think about the people you genuinely admire. Is it because of what they own? Or who they are?

- You respect someone for their kindness, intelligence, or generosity.
- Rarely do you respect someone just because they own a nice car.

Stuff doesn't create respect. Character does.

Case Study: The Quiet Neighbor

I once met a man who drove an old Toyota even though he could easily afford a luxury car.

When I asked why, he said:

"If I drive a fancy car, people might be impressed for ten seconds.

If I live a good life, they might respect me forever."

That stuck with me.

Part III – The Cycle of Showing Off

There's a trap here. When we try to buy respect, we usually end up:

1. Spending money to impress people
2. Those people don't notice or care
3. We feel invisible
4. We try harder with even bigger purchases

It's a **never-ending cycle**.

The Comparison Trap

Even if people do notice, it's fleeting.

Because as soon as someone else buys something bigger, you're back at square one.

There's always someone richer.

There's always someone flashier.

You can't win a race where the finish line keeps moving.

Part IV – The Social Media Amplifier

Social media has made this worse.

- Instagram shows us highlight reels of people's lives.
- We start to think everyone else is richer, prettier, and happier.
- So, we spend to keep up.

But most of those images are illusions. People post their best moments, not their real lives.

Case Study: The Luxury Illusion

Research has found that many luxury car owners are under financial stress.

They bought the car to project an image, not because they could comfortably afford it.

On Instagram, it looks like wealth.

In reality, it's a monthly payment that causes anxiety.

Part V – What Do We Really Want?

At its core, when we buy a flashy car or a big house, what we're really buying is **a story.**

The story says:

- "I am successful."
- "I am worthy of admiration."

But here's the irony:

The fastest way to be admired is not to buy admiration—it's to stop needing it.

Real Respect vs. Perceived Respect

- **Perceived respect:** What you think others feel when they see your possessions.
- **Real respect:** What people actually feel because of your actions and character.

One is shallow and temporary. The other lasts a lifetime.

Part VI – Why People Actually Respect You

Let's do a thought experiment:

Think of the three people you respect most.

Chances are, it's because of:

- How they treat people
- How they carry themselves during tough times
- The value they create for others

Not because of their car.

Case Study: The Mentor

I once worked with a mentor who quietly helped dozens of people launch their careers. He was modest, unassuming, and didn't own anything flashy.

The respect he had was so deep that when he walked into a room, people listened. Not because of wealth, but because of **how he made people feel.**

Part VII – The Freedom of Not Impressing Anyone

Here's the liberating truth:

You don't need to impress anyone.

The moment you stop trying to win approval through possessions is the moment you start living on your own terms.

Practical Ways to Shift the Focus

1. **Ask yourself:** "Am I buying this for me or for them?"
2. **Invest in experiences, not symbols.**
3. **Measure success by freedom, not applause.**

Part VIII – How to Actually Build Influence

Ironically, the people who gain the most admiration are those who focus on **impact, not image**.

- Help others.
- Share knowledge.
- Be generous with time and resources.
- Live authentically.

Those qualities earn the kind of respect that a sports car never will.

Case Study: The Unseen Wealthy

Thomas Stanley's classic book *The Millionaire Next Door* revealed that most millionaires:

- Drive used cars
- Live in modest homes

- Rarely display their wealth

They have real wealth, but they don't need to show it. And because they're not trying to impress, they actually end up being admired more.

Think About This

Before moving on, reflect on these questions:

1. Am I trying to buy respect, or am I building it?
2. Who am I trying to impress—and why?
3. If no one could see what I owned, how would I live differently?

Closing Thought

The "man in the car" paradox is simple:

When people look at a flashy car, they don't admire the driver. They imagine **themselves** in the car.

So, stop chasing admiration that can't be bought. Build a life that earns respect, with or without the car.

Table – Image vs. Reality

Goal (Buying a Luxury Item)	Expected Result	Actual Result
Admiration	"People will respect me"	"People think about themselves"

CHAPTER 9 - Wealth Is What You Don't See

Walk into a neighborhood full of million-dollar homes and you might think,

"Wow, these people are rich."

But here's the uncomfortable truth:

You have no idea how wealthy someone is by looking at what they own.

Because wealth isn't what you see.

Wealth is what you **don't** see.

Part I – The Illusion of Visible Wealth

Visible wealth is easy to fake:

- A leased car
- A mortgaged house
- Designer clothes bought with credit

Anyone can **look** rich for a while.

But real wealth is **invisible**: savings, investments, assets, ownership.

Case Study: The Two Families

Two families live on the same street:

- **Family A:** Big house, luxury cars, expensive vacations. They appear wealthy.
- **Family B:** Modest house, older cars, quiet lifestyle.

Ten years later:

- Family A is drowning in debt.
- Family B quietly retired early.

Why? Because Family B focused on building wealth, not looking wealthy.

Why We Confuse Wealth with Stuff

The human brain craves visible signals.

- You can see a car.
- You can see a watch.
- You can see a big house.

You **can't** see an investment portfolio or a paid-off mortgage.

So, we confuse **displayed wealth** with **actual wealth**.

Psychological Trap: Signaling

We buy things partly to signal success to others. This is natural. But it's also dangerous. When signaling becomes the goal, it competes with the very thing that creates wealth: **saving**.

Part II – The Invisibility of Savings

Think about this:

When someone lives below their means, you don't see it.

- You don't see the vacations they *didn't* take.
- You don't see the cars they *didn't* buy.
- You don't see the stress they *don't* have.

Wealth is built quietly in bank accounts and investment portfolios.

And that's why we underestimate it.

Case Study: The Stealth Millionaire

A janitor named Ronald Read died in 2014 at age 92. He left behind an $8 million fortune.

How?

- He lived simply.

- He saved and invested for decades.
- He never felt the need to display wealth.

His wealth was invisible—until the day he died.

Part III – Spending vs. Building

Here's a simple but powerful truth:

Every dollar you spend is a dollar you no longer have.

Spending shows the world that you had money.
Saving shows the world nothing—but it leaves you with money.

The Cycle of Showiness

Many people believe they can "have it all":

- Spend lavishly today
- Save enough for tomorrow

But the math rarely works that way. In reality, **you have to choose.**

- Spend for status now, or
- Build wealth quietly for freedom later.

The Cost of Looking Rich

When you spend to look rich, you pay twice:

1. With the money itself.
2. With the lost opportunity for that money to grow.

A $100,000 luxury car isn't just $100,000. It's $100,000 **plus decades of lost compounding**.

Case Study: The House that Ate Retirement

A couple I once advised bought the biggest house they could afford because they wanted to show success.

- Their mortgage payments consumed most of their income.
- They couldn't save.
- When a recession hit, they had to sell at a loss.

Their dream home became their financial prison.

Part IV – The Wealth Formula

Wealth = **Income – Ego**

The higher your ego, the more you feel the need to display success.

The more you display, the less wealth you actually build.

What You Don't See

- The frugal family that quietly saves 50% of their income.
- The single parent who prioritizes a college fund over luxury.
- The entrepreneur who reinvests profits instead of buying a sports car.

You don't see these people, because real wealth doesn't make a sound.

Invisible Success Stories

Most long-term wealth builders:

- Drive average cars
- Live in average homes
- Wear average clothes

Not because they can't afford more, but because **they value financial security over status signals**.

Case Study: The Modest Billionaire

Warren Buffett still lives in the house he bought in 1958. He could afford a palace, but he doesn't see the need.

His wealth isn't in what you see. It's in what you **don't**.

Part V – Changing How You See Wealth

1. Don't Judge by Appearances

If you see someone driving an expensive car, don't assume they're wealthy.

They might be—but they also might be broke.

2. Focus on Assets, Not Stuff

Ask yourself: *How much am I building that I can't see?*

3. Redefine Success

Success isn't about impressing strangers.

It's about controlling your time and living without financial stress.

Practical Shift: Show Less, Build More

Before buying something for status, ask:

- Am I buying this for me or for other people?
- Will this purchase bring me closer to freedom—or further away?

The Paradox of Quiet Wealth

Here's the paradox:

- People who quietly build wealth often end up with **more freedom, respect, and options** than those who spend to look wealthy.

- And because they don't feel the need to prove anything, they often enjoy life more.

Case Study: The Low-Profile Investor

I know an investor who could easily live like a billionaire. Instead, he wears simple clothes, drives a normal car, and focuses on his work.

He told me:

"My net worth gives me freedom. Why would I trade that freedom for a bigger car payment?"

Think About This

1. What percentage of my spending is about showing others that I'm doing well?
2. If no one could see what I owned, how would I spend differently?

3. Am I more focused on *appearing* wealthy or *being* wealthy?

Closing Thought

Wealth is what you **don't** see:

- The freedom to say no
- The peace of mind that comes from security
- The options that come from having choices

Stuff is temporary. Wealth is invisible until you need it.

The next time you see someone showing off, remember: **The people with the most to prove usually have the least to show.**

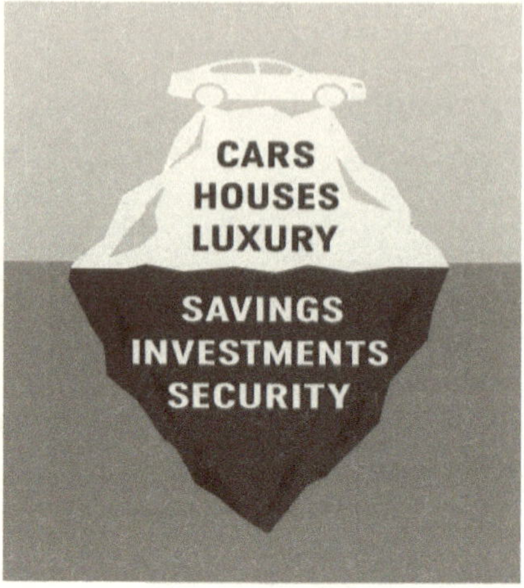

Table – Visible vs. Invisible Wealth

Visible Wealth	Invisible Wealth
Luxury car	Paid-off mortgage
Designer clothes	Emergency fund
Expensive vacations	Investment portfolio

CHAPTER 10

Save Money

There's a secret to building wealth that almost no one talks about:

You don't need a high income to be financially secure.

You need a high savings rate.

Part I – Why Saving Matters More Than You Think

People love to talk about investing, stocks, real estate, and side hustles.

But the single most important factor in building wealth is **how much you keep, not how much you earn**.

If you earn a lot but spend it all, you're not wealthy—you're just busy.

Case Study: Two Friends, Two Outcomes

- **James** earns $250,000 a year, spends nearly all of it on a luxury lifestyle, and saves almost nothing.
- **Maria** earns $80,000 a year, saves 30% of her income, and lives modestly.

Ten years later, Maria is far wealthier than James.

Why? Because **Maria's savings gave her options.**

The Flexibility of Saving

Saving doesn't just build wealth. It gives you **choices**.

- You can take a career risk.
- You can quit a job you hate.
- You can handle emergencies without panic.

Every dollar saved is a dollar of freedom.

The Psychological Benefit

When you have savings, you sleep better.

You stop making decisions out of fear.

You can afford to think long-term.

Part II – The Myth of High Income

People often assume that a higher income automatically equals wealth.

But that's only true if your spending stays low.

In reality:

- **A modest income with a high savings rate beats a big income with a low savings rate.**

Example: The Savings Math

- A household earning $80,000 that saves 30% is saving $24,000 per year.

- A household earning $200,000 that saves 5% is saving $10,000 per year.

Who's building wealth faster?

Why Saving Is Hard

Saving is simple. But it's not easy.

Why? Because of three traps:

1. **Lifestyle inflation** – As income goes up, spending goes up.
2. **Comparison** – We spend to keep up with others.
3. **Impatience** – We want immediate rewards instead of long-term security.

Case Study: The Paycheck Trap

I once met a doctor earning $400,000 a year who said,

"I feel broke."

How could that be?

Every raise came with a bigger house, a nicer car, and more obligations.

By the time the paycheck arrived, it was already spoken for.

Part III – How to Actually Save More

Here are five strategies that work:

1. Pay Yourself First

Automate your savings. Treat it like a bill you owe yourself.

2. Increase Savings with Raises

When your income goes up, keep your spending flat for a year. Save the difference.

3. Avoid Lifestyle Creep

Remember: You don't need to upgrade everything just because you can.

4. Define "Enough"

As discussed earlier: Without a clear definition of "enough," spending will always expand to fill your income.

5. Use "Why" Filters

Before making a purchase, ask:

- Why do I want this?
- Will it actually make me happier—or just impress others?

The Role of Frugality

Frugality isn't about deprivation. It's about **alignment**:

- Spending on what matters most.
- Cutting ruthlessly on what doesn't.

Case Study: The Frugal Millionaire

A couple I know saves over 40% of their income. They still travel, but they cut unnecessary expenses:

- No expensive cable packages
- Cook at home
- Drive cars until they die

They look average on the outside. They are millionaires on the inside.

Part IV – Saving is an investment

People often say, "You can't save your way to wealth—you have to invest."

That's only partly true.

Saving is the foundation.

You can't invest money you haven't saved. And the more you save, the more you can invest when opportunities arise.

Emergency Funds = Confidence

An emergency fund is like a shock absorber for life. It turns a crisis into an inconvenience.

Dry Powder for Opportunity

Having cash on hand means you can:

- Buy stocks when the market crashes
- Start a business when the timing is right
- Say yes to opportunities others can't afford

The Hidden Value of Saving: Time

The more you save, the faster you can reach financial independence.

Imagine saving 50% of your income:

- You only need to work for 15–20 years before you can afford to stop.
- Every dollar saved shortens the time until you own your day.

Part V – Redefining Success

Our culture often praises people for **how much they earn**.

But the real question is:

How much of what you earn do you keep?

- A $60,000 earner who saves 30% may be far more successful than a $200,000 earner who saves nothing.

- Wealth isn't about income. It's about **freedom**.

Case Study: The Self-Made Saver

I met a woman in her 30s who was able to take a year off work to travel the world. She wasn't rich. She just saved 40% of her modest salary for ten years.

Her savings bought her a year of freedom—something a high earner with no savings could never afford.

The Anti-Fragile Mindset

Savings make you **resilient**.

Life will always throw surprises at you:

- Job loss
- Health issues
- Market crashes

Savings give you the power to **bend without breaking**.

Saving Without Shame

Some people are embarrassed to be frugal. They fear looking "cheap."

But ask yourself:

- Would you rather look rich or be rich?
- Would you rather impress strangers or build freedom for yourself?

Reflection Prompt: What Would More Savings Buy You?

Think about this:

- If you doubled your savings rate, what would that allow you to do in 5 years?

- How would your life change if you had a year of expenses saved?

Write it down. It's motivating.

Practical Action Plan

1. **Calculate Your Savings Rate**

   Savings ÷ Income = %.

2. **Set a Target**

   Start with 10%. Move toward 20%, 30%, or even 40%.

3. **Automate It**

   Direct a percentage of each paycheck into savings or investment accounts.

4. **Review Annually**

   Each year, aim to increase your savings rate.

Think About This

1. If I lost my job tomorrow, how many months could I survive?
2. Am I spending money to impress others—or to build freedom?
3. How can I automate saving so it happens even when I'm not thinking about it?

Closing Thought

Saving money is not a punishment.

It's a **gift to your future self.**

Every dollar saved buys:

- Options
- Peace of mind

- The ability to walk away from things that don't serve you

If you want to change your relationship with money, start here.

Before you invest in anything else, invest in saving.

Table 10 – Savings Impact

Savings Rate	Years to Financial Independence (approx.)
10%	50+ years
30%	28 years
50%	15–20 years

CHAPTER 11 - Reasonable > Rational

If personal finance were purely logical, everyone would follow the same plan:

- Maximize returns
- Minimize risk
- Follow formulas
- Retire comfortably

But that's not how it works.

Because we're not robots.

We're human beings with feelings, fears, habits, and biases.

That's why the **best financial plan isn't the most rational—it's the one you can stick with.**

Part I – Why Rational Doesn't Work for Humans

A perfectly rational plan assumes:

- You can predict the future
- You'll never panic
- You'll always act in your best interest

But real life doesn't work that way.

- Markets crash.
- Fear takes over.
- Our goals change.

If you can't stick to a plan in those moments, it doesn't matter how perfect the math looked on paper.

Case Study: The Panic Seller

During the 2008 financial crisis, a man I knew had a "perfect" investment portfolio.

When the market fell 40%, he panicked and sold everything.

On paper, he had the right plan.

In reality, he couldn't emotionally handle the pain.

His perfect plan failed because it wasn't **reasonable**.

Reasonable Plans Are Stickable Plans

Reasonable plans:

- Acknowledge that emotions drive decisions
- Prioritize endurance over optimization
- Build in flexibility for human nature

They might be slightly less "efficient" in theory, but they work better in practice because people actually follow them.

Part II – How Reasonable Looks Different

1. Diversification That Lets You Sleep at Night

A purely rational investor might say:

"Maximize returns by going 100% stocks."

A reasonable investor says:

"I want enough in bonds or cash so that I can sleep through market crashes."

2. Debt Repayment

Rationally, you should pay off the highest-interest debt first. Reasonably, many people start with the smallest debt because it gives a quick psychological win.

This "debt snowball" approach works because it **keeps people motivated.**

3. Over-Insurance

From a math perspective, buying insurance for low-probability events isn't optimal.

From a human perspective, insurance buys peace of mind—and that's worth something.

Case Study: Paying Off a Mortgage Early

Financially, it can make sense to keep a low-interest mortgage and invest the extra money.

But many people pay off their mortgage early because it gives them:

- A sense of safety
- Freedom from debt
- Simplicity

That's not irrational.

It's **reasonable**.

Part III – The Emotional Side of Money

Money decisions aren't made in spreadsheets.

They're made at the dinner table, in the car, and lying awake at night.

This is why **the right answer mathematically isn't always the right answer emotionally.**

The Goal of Money

The goal isn't to beat everyone else in returns. The goal is to **live a life you enjoy and can sustain without panic.**

If a slightly less efficient plan gets you there with peace of mind, it's the right plan.

Part IV – Examples of Reasonable Over Rational

1. Keeping Cash

Cash earns little. It loses value to inflation over time.

So, why do people hold so much?

Because **cash is confidence.**

It gives you the ability to handle emergencies, seize opportunities, and avoid panic.

2. Avoiding the Hottest Investments

Chasing hot stocks might be rational if you think you can pick winners.

But it's not reasonable because:

- It's stressful
- It encourages emotional reactions
- Few people can actually do it well

Index funds are boring but reasonable—and that's why they work.

3. Not Always Maximizing Every Dollar

A rational plan tries to optimize every dollar.

But that can be exhausting.

A reasonable plan allows for small pleasures—dinners out, vacations—because those keep you motivated to stick with your plan long-term.

Part V – How to Build a Reasonable Plan

Step 1: Know Yourself

Ask:

- How much risk can I really tolerate?
- What stresses me out financially?
- What financial mistakes do I tend to repeat?

Step 2: Plan for Behavior, Not Just Math

Your plan should answer:

- How will I handle fear during a crash?
- What safety nets do I need to stay calm?
- How can I avoid decisions I'll regret?

Step 3: Keep It Simple

Complicated plans look good on paper but are easy to abandon.

Simple plans may be less efficient, but they're easier to stick with.

Case Study: The Boring Investor

I know an investor who has built significant wealth by:

- Saving consistently

- Investing in a few broad index funds
- Never checking his portfolio during downturns

He's not chasing "perfect." He's chasing "doable."

Over time, **doable beats perfect.**

The Danger of Over-Optimizing

When you try to squeeze every drop of efficiency out of your finances, you leave no margin for error.

And when something goes wrong, the plan collapses.

Reasonable Includes Flexibility

A reasonable plan leaves room for:

- Market surprises
- Life changes

- Emotions

It allows you to adjust without abandoning everything.

Part VI – Why "Good Enough" Beats "Perfect"

In money—and in life— "good enough" consistently applied for decades is far more powerful than a perfect plan that collapses in a crisis.

- A 90% perfect plan followed forever beats a 100% perfect plan followed for five years.
- Endurance matters more than optimization.

Reflection Prompt

Think about this:

- What financial habits would you keep even if they weren't mathematically perfect, because they keep you motivated?

Write them down. These are your "anchors."

Think About This

1. Is my financial plan built for spreadsheets or for real life?
2. Does my plan assume I'll never panic?
3. Am I chasing "perfect" when I should be chasing "doable"?

Closing Thought

Money is not a math test.

It's a behavior test.

A reasonable plan that you stick with for decades will always beat a perfect plan you abandon in a panic.

In personal finance, good enough is great.

Table 11 – Rational vs. Reasonable

Rational (Theory)	Reasonable (Practice)
Perfectly optimized	Slightly imperfect
Ignores emotion	Acknowledges emotion
Hard to stick with	Sustainable for decades

Chapter 12 - Surprise!

If there's one thing you can count on in life, it's that **things won't go the way you expect.**

Part I – Why the Future Always Surprises Us

Look back 20 years.

How many of the biggest events in your life—and in the world—could you have predicted?

- The financial crisis of 2008
- The rise of social media
- A global pandemic in 2020
- Cryptocurrency
- Wars that reshaped entire economies

Almost none of these things were on anyone's radar until they happened.

And yet, when we plan for the future, we act as if the next 20 years will unfold neatly according to our expectations.

Case Study: The 2020 Pandemic

In early 2020, virtually no one included "global lockdown" in their financial plan.

Within months:

- Jobs disappeared
- Supply chains broke
- Markets crashed and then soared
- Entire industries shifted overnight

This is a reminder: **the biggest risks and opportunities are almost always the ones you didn't see coming.**

The Illusion of Prediction

We love predictions because they make us feel safe.

- Economists predict growth rates.
- Analysts predict stock prices.
- Planners predict retirement dates.

But history shows us that **we're terrible at predicting the future.**

Why We Overestimate Our Predictive Power

1. **Hindsight bias:** After something happens, we tell ourselves we "saw it coming."
2. **Overconfidence:** We believe the future will look like the past.
3. **Desire for certainty:** We crave a story that makes the world feel predictable.

Part II – Planning for Surprise

The solution isn't to predict the future perfectly. It's to **build plans that can handle surprises.**

Room for Error

Think of your financial life like building a bridge. Engineers don't design bridges to carry the exact weight they expect. They add **margins of safety** in case something unexpected happens.

You should do the same with money.

Case Study: The Conservative Saver

I once worked with a couple who always saved more than they needed.

Friends teased them for being "overly cautious."

But when one of them faced a sudden medical crisis, their savings absorbed the shock.

They didn’t have to sell their house.

They didn’t have to panic.

Surprises didn’t break them because they planned for them.

The Problem with History as a Guide

We often plan for the future by looking at history.

- “The stock market averages 10% returns.”
- “Real estate always goes up over decades.”

But history is only a guide to the **average** of what has happened—not the **specifics** of what will happen next.

History Doesn't Repeat; It Rhymes

World War II was a surprise.

The oil crisis of the 1970s was a surprise.

The dot-com bubble was a surprise.

The **specifics** are always different.

The **pattern** is that surprises happen.

Part III – How to Plan for the Unknown

1. Expect Volatility

Volatility is not a bug of investing—it's a feature. If markets were predictable, there would be no reward for taking risk.

2. Build a Margin of Safety

- Keep extra savings.
- Don't spend to the edge of your income.

- Avoid leverage that leaves no room for error.

3. Plan to Be Wrong

Ask yourself:

- "What if I'm wrong about my assumptions?"
- "What happens if things take twice as long as I expect?"

4. Avoid All-or-Nothing Bets

Spreading your investments ensures that no single surprise can wipe you out.

Case Study: The Diversified Investor

I know a man who invests conservatively, even when the market looks strong.

People ask why he doesn't "go all in" to maximize returns.

His answer:

"I want to make sure that if I'm wrong about one thing, it doesn't ruin me."

This mindset has kept him financially calm through multiple crises.

Part IV – The Positive Side of Surprise

Not all surprises are bad.

- The internet was a surprise.
- The smartphone was a surprise.
- Medical breakthroughs are surprises.

Positive surprises can completely change your trajectory, too.

Case Study: The Accidental Career

A woman I know started a small blog as a hobby. It unexpectedly took off, turned into a business, and allowed her to leave a job she disliked.

This was never part of her plan.

But because she created options, she could take advantage of the surprise.

Optionality: The Power to Pivot

The best way to prepare for positive surprises is to:

- Save aggressively
- Stay curious
- Keep learning

When the world changes, you'll be ready to adapt instead of clinging to a plan that no longer fits.

Part V – Surprises Are Normal

The truth is, surprises **aren't rare**. They're constant.

What feels like a "shock" in the moment often becomes the new normal within a few years.

The Danger of Rigid Plans

Plans that are too rigid assume:

- The world will stay the same
- You will stay the same
- Your goals will stay the same

But none of those are true.

A rigid plan can break the moment reality doesn't match your script.

The Flexible Plan

A flexible plan says:

- "I expect to be surprised."
- "I will adjust as needed."
- "I will not risk ruin just to squeeze out a little more return."

Reflection Prompt: What If…?

Write down three "what if" scenarios:

1. What if I lost my job tomorrow?
2. What if markets crashed 40%?
3. What if my goals change in 10 years?

Then write down how you would handle them.

Think About This

1. Does my financial plan assume the future will look like the past?
2. Do I have enough margin to handle surprises without panic?
3. Am I ready for positive surprises as much as negative ones?

Closing Thought

The world will surprise you.

It always has, and it always will.

Your job is not to predict.

Your job is to prepare.

If you expect the unexpected, you'll never be shocked. You'll just be ready.

Table 12 – Rigid vs. Flexible Planning

Rigid Planning	Flexible Planning
Assumes no surprises	Expects surprises
Breaks under stress	Bends under stress
All-or-nothing bets	Diversified and cautious

Chapter 13 - Room for Error

When engineers design a bridge to carry 10,000 pounds, they don't build it to carry exactly 10,000 pounds.

They build it to carry 30,000 pounds.

That extra capacity is called a **margin of safety**.

It's the buffer that allows for mistakes, unexpected stress, and conditions that weren't part of the original plan.

In money, **room for error** is your financial margin of safety.

Part I – Why We Need Margin

Most people plan their financial life as if the future will unfold in a straight line.

But the world doesn't work that way.

- Jobs get lost.
- Markets crash.

- Health changes.
- Surprises appear out of nowhere.

Room for error is how you **survive the surprises.**

Case Study: The Tightrope Walker

Imagine someone walking across a tightrope without a net. Even a small slip can be fatal.

Now imagine someone doing the same walk with a safety net.

A slip is still inconvenient—but it's not catastrophic.

Margin of safety is that net.

The Cost of Living on the Edge

When there's no room for error:

- A single mistake can ruin years of work.

- Small surprises become major crises.
- You live in a constant state of anxiety.

Case Study: The Over-Leveraged Investor

In 2007, many investors borrowed huge amounts of money to buy real estate.

On paper, it was a brilliant plan.

But when the market collapsed in 2008, they had no cushion.

Banks foreclosed. Fortunes vanished.

It wasn't just bad luck—it was **a lack of margin**.

Part II – How to Build Room for Error

1. Keep More Cash Than You Think You Need

Cash isn't exciting. It doesn't earn much.

But it gives you time and flexibility when things go wrong.

2. Avoid Excessive Debt

Debt magnifies everything: gains and losses.

Without margin, debt can turn a small setback into bankruptcy.

3. Diversify

Diversification isn't about maximizing gains.

It's about **minimizing the chance of ruin**.

4. Plan for Multiple Outcomes

Ask yourself:

- What if I'm wrong?
- What if things take twice as long?
- What if the worst-case scenario happens?

Case Study: NASA and Redundancy

NASA builds redundancy into spacecraft.

- Multiple backup systems.
- Extra fuel.
- Alternate routes.

Because when things go wrong in space, there's no room for improvisation.

Apply that same thinking to your finances.

Part III – Why Margin Feels "Boring"

In good times, margin feels like wasted potential:

- Holding extra cash feels "lazy."
- Diversifying feels like you're missing out on bigger gains.
- Avoiding risk feels slow.

But in bad times, margin feels like genius.

The Emotional Benefit

Margin isn't just financial—it's psychological.

When you know you have a buffer, you:

- Sleep better
- Make calmer decisions
- Avoid panic selling or desperate actions

Part IV – Room for Error Is Freedom

When you have room for error, you can:

- Take risks in your career
- Start a business
- Try new things

Because you know that a single mistake won't wipe you out.

Case Study: The Flexible Entrepreneur

An entrepreneur I know saved aggressively before starting her company.

Her peers jumped straight in with borrowed money.

When her first idea didn't work, she had the cushion to pivot.

Her peers didn't. Most of them went bankrupt.

Room for error gave her **options**.

Why We Resist Margin

Our culture rewards efficiency.

- "Put your money to work."
- "Leverage your assets."
- "Maximize returns."

But maximum efficiency often means **zero resilience**.

The Problem with Perfection

If your plan only works when everything goes perfectly, you don't have a plan—you have a wish.

Part V – How Much Margin Do You Need?

There's no exact formula, but here are guidelines:

1. **Cash:** 6–12 months of living expenses (more if self-employed).
2. **Investments:** Diversify across asset classes.
3. **Debt:** Keep fixed expenses low enough that a surprise won't sink you.
4. **Career:** Maintain skills that can adapt to new jobs or industries.

Reflection Prompt: Where's My Safety Net?

Ask yourself:

- What's my plan if I'm wrong?
- How long can I survive without income?
- Where is my financial safety net thin?

Part VI – The Humility of Margin

Room for error is an admission:

"I don't know what the future holds."

That humility is a superpower.

It protects you from overconfidence and from risks you didn't see coming.

Case Study: Buffett's Cash Pile

Warren Buffett often holds billions in cash.

Critics say he could earn more if he invested it all.

But that cash gives him flexibility when others are forced to sell.

It's a margin of safety that lets him act from strength, not desperation.

Margin Turns Chaos into Opportunity

When you have a buffer:

- A crisis becomes an opportunity to invest
- A layoff becomes a chance to change direction
- A setback becomes a speed bump, not a dead end

Think About This

1. If I lost my job tomorrow, how long could I stay afloat?
2. Does my financial life assume everything will go right?
3. Am I leaving enough room for error in my plans?

Closing Thought

You don't build wealth by being perfect.
You build wealth by **surviving long enough to let compounding work.**

Margin of safety is the difference between being fragile and being resilient.

In money—as in engineering—the strongest structures are the ones that can handle the unexpected.

Table 13 – Life With vs. Without Margin

Without Margin	With Margin
One mistake = disaster	One mistake = recovery
Constant stress	Calm confidence
No flexibility	Ability to pivot

Chapter 14 - You'll Change

Think back to who you were 10 years ago.

What did you care about? What were your goals? Who did you want to be?

Now ask yourself: **how many of those goals still matter today?**

Part I – The Illusion of a Fixed Future

When we plan for the future, we assume that the person we'll be in 30 years will want exactly what we want today.

But psychology research shows something called the **end of history illusion**:

- We believe we've changed a lot in the past.
- We believe we won't change much in the future.
- We are almost always wrong.

You are not done changing.

And that has huge implications for your money.

Case Study: The Doctor Who Wanted Out

In his twenties, a man dreamed of becoming a doctor. He spent a decade in medical school and residency.

By his mid-forties, he was burned out. He wanted to leave medicine and start a winery.

But he couldn't. His entire financial plan was built around staying in medicine forever.

He had trapped himself by planning for a version of himself that no longer existed.

Why Goals Evolve

Your priorities shift as you go through different stages of life:

- **20s:** Adventure, experience, proving yourself
- **30s:** Stability, family, career building
- **40s:** Meaning, balance, health
- **50s+:** Freedom, legacy, time

What feels urgent today may be irrelevant tomorrow.

Part II – The Danger of Over-Specific Plans

Many people make financial plans with **rigid precision**:

- "I will work in this career forever."
- "I will retire at 60."
- "I will live in this city."

But life rarely sticks to the script.

Case Study: The Corporate Exit

I knew a woman who planned her entire life around climbing the corporate ladder.

At 38, she was exhausted and wanted to quit.

Her plan had assumed a lifetime of promotions and raises. She had no flexibility for a change of heart.

The Cost of Locking Yourself In

When you build a financial life that **requires** everything to go exactly as planned:

- You have no room to pivot.
- You become a prisoner of your own past goals.

Part III – Flexible Goals for a Changing You

A better approach:

- Save and invest in a way that gives you **options.**
- Avoid committing to a future that hasn't arrived yet.

The Power of Options

Think of financial planning like buying options:

- **Cash savings:** The option to leave a bad job.
- **Diversified investments:** The option to take a risk without ruin.
- **Low fixed expenses:** The option to downshift without fear.

Part IV – Humility About the Future

It's not that planning is pointless. Planning is crucial. But your plans must be **humble**:

- Assume you don't know what future-you will want.
- Build a life flexible enough to adapt when you change your mind.

Case Study: The Early Retiree Who Returned to Work

I know someone who worked for 20 years, saved aggressively, and retired at 42.

Within two years, he was back at work—not because he needed money, but because he missed the challenge and community.

His plan was flexible. Retirement wasn't a cage; it was a choice.

Why "Purpose" Matters More Than "Plan"

A plan answers, "What will I do?"

Purpose answers, "What matters to me?"

When you know your purpose, you can adapt your plan as you grow.

Part V – The Slow Drift of Values

This is why some people who obsess over retirement numbers are shocked when they reach their goal and realize:

- They no longer want the same things.
- They value health and relationships over possessions.
- The goalpost moved.

Reflection Prompt: How Have You Already Changed?

Think about your 20-year-old self:

- Would that version of you recognize who you are today?
- What did you think would make you happy back then?
- What do you value now instead?

This exercise reminds you that **future-you will be just as different.**

Part VI – Building Financial Plans for a Moving Target

1. Save for Flexibility, Not Just for a Goal

Instead of saying "I need $2 million to retire at 60," say:

- "I want to build enough wealth that I can make changes whenever I want."

2. Avoid Golden Handcuffs

Don't let a lifestyle lock you into a job you hate. Low fixed expenses = high flexibility.

3. Keep Learning

Skills are financial assets. The more you learn, the easier it is to pivot.

4. Allow for "Mini Experiments"

Try small lifestyle changes before committing:

- Move to a new city for a few months.
- Test a side business before quitting your job.

- Take a sabbatical before full retirement.

Case Study: The Experimenter

A friend of mine thought he wanted to live abroad permanently.

Instead of selling everything, he rented an apartment in Spain for six months.

Halfway through, he realized it wasn't for him.

His experiment saved him from a permanent decision based on a temporary desire.

Part VII – Financial Independence as a Moving Goalpost

The ultimate purpose of financial independence is **not retirement**.

It's **control**:

- Control to change your mind.
- Control to say yes or no.
- Control to live life on your terms as you evolve.

Why This Is Hard to Accept

Our brains crave certainty.

We want a clear picture of what life will look like 30 years from now.

But **the only certainty is that you will change.**

The Paradox of Success

The more you grow, the more your goals change.

Success itself changes what you want.

Think About This

1. How have my goals changed in the last 10 years?
2. Am I leaving space in my plans for future-me to want something different?
3. What decisions am I making today that assume I'll stay the same forever?

Closing Thought

You will change.

Your priorities will change.

Your definition of "enough" will change.

The best financial plan doesn't try to lock you into today's version of yourself.

It builds **options for the person you haven't become yet.**

Table – Fixed vs. Flexible Plans

Fixed Plan	**Flexible Plan**
Assumes you never change	Expects you to change
Locks you into choices	Creates options
Can become a trap	Adapts as you grow

Chapter 15 - Nothing's Free

In life, everything has a cost.

Sometimes it's a price tag.

Other times, it's invisible.

In money, **there's no such thing as a free lunch.**

- High returns? They come with volatility.
- Safety? It comes with lower returns.
- Opportunity? It comes with risk.

The trick is not to avoid paying a price.

It's to **make sure you're paying the right price knowingly.**

Part I – The Hidden Cost of Everything

When you see an investment returning 12% per year, you might think:

"That's amazing. It's practically free money!"

But that return isn't free. The price is:

- Staying invested through market crashes
- Watching your portfolio drop 30% and not panicking
- Enduring uncertainty

The problem is that most people don't realize this **is the price**—until the bill comes due.

Case Study: The Market Crash

During the 2008 crash, many investors who thought they could handle risk discovered that the true price of high returns was **emotional pain.**

When the market fell 50%, they sold out. They refused to pay the emotional cost—and missed the recovery.

The Most Important Question in Money

Before making any financial decision, ask:

"What is the real price I will have to pay?"

Part II – Different Prices for Different Goals

High Returns = Volatility

If you want the possibility of double-digit returns, be prepared for:

- Gut-wrenching declines
- Years of nothing
- Uncertainty

Safety = Lower Returns

If you want stability, be prepared to earn less. There's a cost for safety: missed opportunities.

Liquidity = Lower Returns

If you want to be able to access your money at any time, you can't lock it into high-return, illiquid investments.

The Hidden Price: Patience

In investing, **time is a cost.**

You pay for compounding with patience.

Most people underestimate how hard it is to sit still for years.

Case Study: The Bored Investor

I know an investor who bought an index fund in 2009. After five years of slow, steady growth, he sold because "it wasn't moving fast enough."

He paid the cost of impatience—and missed the best decade of returns.

Part III – You Can't Avoid the Price

The cost is there whether you acknowledge it or not.

- If you want high growth, you pay with volatility.
- If you want safety, you pay with lower growth.
- If you want quick results, you pay by giving up long-term gains.

The Market's Way of Charging You

Markets don't send you a bill.

They send you:

- Uncertainty
- Fear
- Stress

That's the price.

Most people abandon their plan because they don't like how the bill is presented.

Part IV – What Are You Willing to Pay For?

When you understand that nothing is free, you can decide what price you're willing to pay.

- Are you willing to endure volatility for long-term wealth?
- Are you willing to give up potential upside for security?
- Are you willing to sacrifice some luxury today for freedom tomorrow?

Case Study: The Safe Saver

A man I know invested only in bonds because he couldn't tolerate stock market swings.

He paid the price of **safety with slow growth**—and that was fine for him.

He could sleep at night.

He knew the price and paid it willingly.

Part V – The Price of Financial Freedom

Financial independence sounds wonderful:

- No boss
- No obligations
- Full control of your time

But even that isn't free. The price is:

- Years of saving

- Sacrifices in the present
- Saying "no" to certain pleasures

Case Study: The Early Retiree

A couple retired at 40.

They live simply, with a modest lifestyle.

They paid the price of **years of discipline** to earn freedom early.

For them, that price was worth it.

The Price of Doing Nothing

Not making a decision also has a cost:

- Keeping all your money in cash means inflation quietly eats it.
- Avoiding risk means losing opportunity.

The Price Tag Nobody Talks About: Stress

There's another hidden cost in money: **stress.**

- Debt carries stress.
- Lack of savings carries stress.
- Risky investments carry stress.

Sometimes it's worth accepting a lower return if it means less stress.

Part VI – Everyone Pays. Choose Wisely.

No matter what path you choose, you will pay:

- With your time
- With your comfort
- With your peace of mind

The key is to **pick the trade-offs that fit you.**

Reflection Prompt: What Price Are You Paying Right Now?

Write down:

1. What costs am I paying for my current lifestyle?
2. What prices am I willing to pay for my future goals?
3. Am I clear on what I'm giving up with each decision?

Why People Get This Wrong

We are wired to look at **visible costs** and ignore invisible ones.

- The price of a luxury car is obvious.
- The price of lost compounding is invisible.
- The price of stress doesn't appear on a receipt—but you still pay it.

Part VII – Learning to Pay Willingly

The best investors accept the bill.

They don't complain when markets fall. They understand that it's just **the cost of admission.**

Case Study: The Patient Investor

A woman I know continued investing through the 2000 tech crash, the 2008 recession, and the 2020 pandemic.

She never stopped contributing.

She understood that volatility wasn't a bug—it was the **price of long-term wealth**.

Think About This

1. What price are you willing to pay for freedom?

2. What price are you unwilling to pay, even if the reward is high?
3. Am I making financial decisions with full awareness of the hidden costs?

Closing Thought

Everything has a cost.

If someone promises you high returns with no risk, they're lying.
If someone promises you security with no trade-offs, they're lying.

Nothing in life is free.

The key is to know the price ahead of time, decide if you're willing to pay it, and then—when the bill comes due—pay it without complaint.

Table 15 – What You Pay For

Goal	Price You Pay
High growth	Volatility, emotional swings
Safety	Lower returns
Quick results	Missed compounding

CHAPTER 16 – You & Me

Money is often treated like a math problem:

"If you just follow these formulas, you'll be fine."

But money is not the same for everyone.

It's shaped by:

- Our upbringing
- Our fears
- Our goals
- Our definition of "enough"

This is why **what works for me may not work for you.**

Part I – Different Games, Different Rules

Imagine two people at the same poker table.

- One is playing to have fun.
- The other is playing to pay their mortgage.

Same game. Different stakes.

If they copy each other's strategies, both will lose.

Money works the same way.

Case Study: The Aggressive Investor

A young, single tech worker invests 90% in stocks. This makes sense for her:

- Long time horizon
- Stable income
- No dependents

Her neighbor, a 60-year-old close to retirement, tries to copy her strategy.

When the market crashes, he panics and sells everything. **Different games. Different goals. Same table.**

The Problem with Advice

People give financial advice based on **their own goals, not yours.**

- A billionaire says, "Just hold forever." Easy for them to say.
- A 25-year-old says, "Take big risks." But that might ruin someone at 55.

There's no universal playbook because there's no universal life.

Part II – The Personal in Personal Finance

Money decisions are less about spreadsheets and more about **values**.

- Do you value freedom over luxury?
- Do you value security over growth?

- Do you value experiences over things?

Your answers to these questions will shape decisions differently than mine.

Reflection Prompt: My Money Priorities

Take five minutes to rank these in order of importance:

1. Freedom
2. Security
3. Comfort
4. Status
5. Growth
6. Generosity

Part III – Why Copying Others Rarely Works

1. Different Backgrounds

A person who grew up in poverty will view risk differently than someone who always felt secure.

2. Different Tolerances

Some people can handle 50% market drops without blinking. Others lose sleep over 5%.

3. Different Goals

If your goal is early retirement at 40, you'll make completely different decisions than someone who loves their work and plans to do it forever.

Case Study: The Two Friends

Two friends graduate college together:

- One dreams of building a big company.
- The other dreams of a quiet, stable life.

If they try to live the same financial life, they'll both be miserable.

Part IV – Understanding Your Game

The first step in managing money well is understanding:

- What game you're playing
- What game others are playing

Avoid Getting Distracted

It's tempting to copy others because it looks like they're "winning."

But if you're not playing their game, their version of winning might be your version of losing.

Part V – The Danger of "Keeping Up"

Keeping up with others is a losing game:

- Their goals are different.
- Their resources are different.
- Their risk tolerance is different.

If you measure your success using someone else's scoreboard, you'll always feel behind.

Case Study: The Neighbor's New Car

Your neighbor buys a luxury car. You start thinking, *Maybe I should upgrade too.*

But you have no idea:

- Whether they paid cash or took out a loan.
- Whether they're prioritizing retirement or appearances.
- Whether that car is actually making them happy.

You are judging your life against incomplete information.

Part VI – How to Play Your Own Game

1. Define Success for Yourself

Write it down. Make it specific.

2. Filter Advice

When someone gives financial advice, ask:

- What game are they playing?
- Does that game match mine?

3. Build a Plan That Fits You

If a plan doesn't fit your values, you won't stick with it. And the best plan is useless if you can't stick with it.

Case Study: The Quiet Planner

I know a man who could chase high returns. Instead, he keeps a balanced portfolio and a modest lifestyle.

Why? Because his goal isn't to be the richest. It's to be calm, content, and flexible.

Part VII – Respecting Different Games

Not only should you avoid copying others—you should avoid judging them.

- The person who spends freely might value experiences over security.
- The person who saves every penny might value security over fun.

Both can be right for their own goals.

The Humility to Say "I Don't Know"

When you see someone making financial decisions that don't make sense to you, remember:

You don't know their game.

Think About This

1. What game am I playing with money?
2. What am I optimizing for?
3. Whose game am I accidentally copying?

Closing Thought

Personal finance is personal.

The only scoreboard that matters is your own.

Once you stop copying other people's moves, you free yourself to play a game you can actually win.

Different games, same table.

Table – My Game vs. Their Game

My Goal	Their Goal
Early retirement	Career growth forever
Security	Maximum wealth
Simplicity	Status

Chapter 17

The Seduction of Pessimism

If you want to sound smart about money, just say:

“This won’t end well.”

You’ll get nods, agreement, and maybe a segment on TV.

Pessimism feels safe. It feels intelligent. It feels responsible.

But the truth is: **pessimism is seductive, while optimism quietly wins.**

Part I – Why Pessimism Sounds So Smart

There are three reasons pessimism is so appealing:

1. **Bad news grabs our attention.**
   We evolved to notice threats. It’s why we doomscroll.

2. **Pessimism has urgency.**

   Bad things tend to happen fast. Good things happen slowly.

3. **Pessimism protects us from disappointment.**

   If you expect the worst, you won't be surprised.

Case Study: The Crash Headlines

During every bull market, headlines warn:

- "The bubble will burst soon."
- "Markets are dangerously overvalued."
- "A major recession is inevitable."

Sometimes they're right—but most of the time, **the market grows anyway.**

Why Optimism Feels Naïve

Optimism doesn't grab attention because it's slow and boring:

- Companies grow gradually.
- People invent new things.
- Standards of living rise.

Optimism requires patience, which doesn't make for a catchy headline.

Part II – The Cost of Pessimism

Constant pessimism leads to:

- Missed opportunities
- Fear-based decisions
- Sitting out of markets for decades

Case Study: The Sideline Saver

I met an investor who kept all his savings in cash from 2009 to 2019 because he was convinced another crash was coming.

The stock market more than tripled in that time. He missed all of it because pessimism felt safer.

Pessimism vs. Optimism Over Time

- **Short term:** Pessimism is louder.
- **Long term:** Optimism wins.

History proves this:

- Despite wars, depressions, and disasters, global wealth has grown dramatically over the last 100 years.
- Life expectancy, technology, and living standards have all improved.

Part III – Why We Fall for Doom

1. Fear Feels Like Wisdom

If someone says, "Be careful, disaster is coming," it feels like they care about you.

2. Media Incentives

Bad news gets clicks.

Good news rarely goes viral.

3. The One Big Crash Bias

People who lived through a crash—like 2008 or 2000—often believe it will happen again soon.

Their scar shapes their entire outlook.

Case Study: The Great Depression Generation

Many who grew up during the Great Depression avoided investing for the rest of their lives.

Even when times changed, their memory of pain kept them pessimistic.

Realistic Optimism

Optimism isn't blind faith that everything will be perfect.

Realistic optimism says:

- Bad things will happen.
- But progress, over time, outweighs setbacks.

The Progress Engine

Look at the past 50 years:

- Medicine: Vaccines, cancer treatments, longer life expectancy.
- Technology: The internet, smartphones, AI.

- Standard of living: Clean water, better housing, global education.

None of this was guaranteed—but it happened because people kept building.

Part IV – The Long View

Investing in progress requires:

- Patience
- Tolerance for setbacks
- Confidence that human creativity tends to solve problems

Case Study: The Pandemic Rebound

In March 2020, markets collapsed as COVID spread. By the end of the year, markets had fully recovered.

Why?

Because innovation—vaccines, remote work tools, adaptation—kicked in faster than anyone predicted.

The Hidden Price of Pessimism

The cost of pessimism is **missed compounding.**

- You save in cash forever, waiting for the "right time."
- That time never comes.
- Decades pass, and opportunities are gone.

Why Optimism Wins

1. **Progress compounds.**

   Small improvements add up.

2. **Setbacks are temporary.**

   Crises happen, but recovery happens too.

3. **The future is built by people who believe things can get better.**

Case Study: The Builder's Mindset

Entrepreneurs, inventors, and long-term investors all share one trait:

They believe that problems can be solved.

That belief drives action, which drives progress.

Balancing Pessimism and Optimism

Being blindly optimistic is dangerous.

Being blindly pessimistic is paralyzing.

The right balance:

- *Short-term caution*
- *Long-term optimism*

Practical Rule: Plan Like a Pessimist, Act Like an Optimist

- Save for emergencies.
- Diversify.
- Avoid debt.

…but once that safety net is in place, **invest in the future.**

Think About This

1. Am I making decisions from fear or from confidence?
2. Have I been sitting on the sidelines waiting for bad news?

3. What evidence of long-term progress am I ignoring?

Closing Thought

The world is messy, unpredictable, and full of setbacks.

But over time, **progress wins.**

Pessimism sounds smart.

Optimism makes you rich.

Table – Pessimism vs. Optimism

Pessimism (Short-Term)	Optimism (Long-Term)
Urgent, loud	Quiet, patient
Protects from pain	Builds wealth

CHAPTER 18 – When You'll Believe Anything

Human beings love stories.

We crave them.

We live by them.

And when it comes to money, **stories often matter more than facts.**

Part I – Why We Believe Stories

When faced with a complex world, our brains look for simple explanations.

- Numbers feel cold.
- Stories feel human.

A good story makes us believe things that data alone never could.

Case Study: The 1990s Tech Boom

In the late 1990s, everyone had a story:

“The internet will change everything. Old rules don’t apply.”

The story was partly true. But it also led to **irrational behavior**:

- Sky-high valuations
- No profits, no business plans—just hype

Data said, “This doesn’t make sense.”

The story said, “This time is different.”

Guess which one people believed?

Part II – The Narrative Fallacy

The narrative fallacy is when we:

- Take random events
- Connect them with a story

- And convince ourselves that the story makes it inevitable

It's a way of imposing order on chaos.

But the world doesn't always work that way.

Why Stories Are Powerful

- Stories stick in our memory.
- They spread easily.
- They trigger emotions.

Numbers rarely do any of those things.

Part III – When Stories Take Over

1. During Booms

In good times, people tell stories of endless opportunity:

- "Housing prices never fall."

- "This stock can only go up."

2. During Busts

In bad times, people tell stories of doom:

- "The market will never recover."
- "This is the end."

Both extremes ignore the messy middle where reality usually lies.

Case Study: The 2020 Market Crash

In March 2020, the dominant story was:

"This is the next Great Depression."

Markets fell 30% in a month.

Then—surprisingly—they recovered within the year.

The story was powerful, but it was wrong.

Why We Prefer Stories Over Probabilities

Probabilities say:

"There's a 20% chance this will happen."

Stories say:

"This WILL happen because…"

Stories feel more certain, even when they're wrong.

Part IV – The Cost of Believing Everything

Overconfidence

When you buy into a story, you stop asking:

- "What if I'm wrong?"
- "What don't I know?"

Bandwagon Behavior

Stories spread fast.

When everyone else believes, we start to believe too—even without evidence.

The Bubble Effect

Most bubbles are built on **stories that were true at first but taken too far**:

- Railroads will change America. (True… in 1850.)
- The internet will change the world. (True… but not every dot-com was worth billions.)
- AI will change everything. (True… but maybe not as fast as people expect.)

Part V – Building a Healthy Skepticism

The goal is not to ignore stories. Stories are powerful and often contain truth.

The goal is to **listen to stories without losing perspective.**

How to Test a Story

1. Does the story rely on "this time is different"?
2. Does the story make me feel certain or excited more than thoughtful?
3. If the story turns out to be wrong, will I still be okay?

Case Study: The Patient Investor

An investor I know listens to market stories all the time.

But instead of reacting, he asks:

- "Does this change my long-term plan?"

If the answer is no, he does nothing. This approach saved him from chasing bubbles—and from panicking during crashes.

Part VI – Stories Aren't Bad

Stories drive:

- Innovation
- Ambition
- Progress

The story of "a better future" is what pushes people to try new things.

But you have to be careful about which stories you buy into.

Why Your Own Story Matters Most

The most powerful financial story is the one you tell yourself:

- Who do I want to be?
- What am I building toward?
- Why am I saving and investing?

If your personal story is strong enough, you won't get distracted by everyone else's.

Reflection Prompt: Write Your Story

Write a one-page version of your money story:

- What do I want from my money?
- What am I willing to do—and not do—to get it?
- What matters more to me than returns?

Think About This

1. What stories am I currently believing about money?
2. Are those stories based on evidence—or just excitement and fear?
3. Am I building my financial life around someone else's story?

Closing Thought

Numbers make you think.

Stories make you act.

The trick is to make sure the story you believe in is one worth living out.

Because in money, the wrong story can cost you everything.

Table 18 – Data vs. Story

Data	Story
Precise	Emotional
Hard to remember	Easy to remember
Slow to act on	Inspires action

PART II – TURNING INSIGHT INTO ACTION

CHAPTER 19: The Psychology of Money in a Few Words

After 18 chapters of stories, research, and reflection, what are we left with?

The patterns are clear.

The core ideas about money can be summarized into **five powerful truths.**

Truth #1: Less Ego, More Wealth

Most people don't get into financial trouble because of bad math.

They get into trouble because of ego.

- Ego says, "I need to look successful right now."
- Ego says, "I need to impress strangers."
- Ego says, "I'm smarter than the market."

Every dollar spent on ego is a dollar not invested in freedom.

Lesson:

Wealth is built by humility.

Reflection Prompt:

- Where in my financial life am I trying to prove something?

Truth #2: Money Buys Time, Not Things

The ultimate purpose of money is to **control your time**. Everything else—cars, houses, status—is secondary.

When you trade time for money, you lose. When you trade money for time, you win.

Lesson:

Design your financial life around flexibility, not possessions.

Reflection Prompt:

- If I had total control of my time, what would I stop doing tomorrow?

Truth #3: Survival > Brilliance

Success in finance isn't about predicting markets perfectly. It's about **not getting wiped out.**

- The best investors aren't the ones with the highest returns in a single year.
- They're the ones who stay in the game the longest.

Room for error, patience, and risk management matter more than genius.

Lesson:

Avoid ruin at all costs.

Reflection Prompt:

- What single event could ruin me financially? Have I planned for it?

Truth #4: Behavior Beats Math

The difference between a "good" financial plan and a "perfect" one is negligible—if you can stick with the good one.

The difference between a "perfect" plan that you abandon and a "good" one you stay with is enormous.

Lesson:

Reasonable beats rational because reasonable lasts.

Reflection Prompt:

- Is my plan designed for spreadsheets or for my emotions?

Truth #5: The Long Game Wins

The biggest results in life and money come from **small actions repeated over long periods of time.**

- Most big wins are the result of compounding.
- Compounding only works when you stay invested long enough to let it run.

Lesson:

Time is your greatest ally. Don't interrupt compounding.

Reflection Prompt:

- Where am I interrupting compounding because I'm impatient?

The Psychology of Money as a Framework

Let's translate the lessons into a **simple, actionable framework**:

1. Save Aggressively

- Saving gives you options.
- The amount you save matters more than how much you earn.
- Build an emergency fund, then keep going.

2. Stay Humble

- Expect to be surprised.
- Diversify.
- Leave room for error.

3. Avoid Complexity

- Simple plans work best.
- Automate good behavior.
- Don't chase fads.

4. Play Your Own Game

- Define your personal goals.
- Ignore what everyone else is doing.
- Personal finance is personal.

5. Value Time Over Status

- Spend less than you earn.
- Buy back your time.
- Measure wealth in flexibility.

What This Looks Like Day-to-Day

A Daily Checklist

1. **Did I spend less than I earned today?**
2. **Did I save or invest something, even a small amount?**
3. **Did I make a decision that future-me will thank me for?**

Simple Rules to Live By

- Avoid big lifestyle inflation.
- Be skeptical of "hot tips."
- Think in decades, not days.
- Don't try to impress people who aren't paying attention.
- Remember: you don't have to be perfect. You just have to endure.

Why Simplicity Wins

It's tempting to think that wealth comes from complexity:

- Sophisticated strategies
- Timing the market
- Insider knowledge

But wealth actually comes from **consistency**:

- Spend less than you earn.
- Invest regularly.
- Be patient.
- Avoid big mistakes.

It's not sexy, but it works.

Case Study Recap: Three Archetypes

The Sprinter

- Takes big risks
- Makes quick gains
- Usually burns out or blows up

The Show-Off

- Spends to look rich
- Rarely builds lasting wealth

The Tortoise

- Saves steadily
- Avoids ruin
- Ends up far ahead

The Final Equation

Wealth = (Behavior × Time) – Ego

The Human Side of Money

Ultimately, this book has been about **people, not finance**.

- How we think about money
- How our experiences shape our decisions
- How emotions, not spreadsheets, determine outcomes

What Really Matters

At the end of your life, you won't care about:

- The exact number in your brokerage account
- How many years you beat the market
- The car you drove

You'll care about:

- Whether you spent your time the way you wanted
- Whether you helped the people you love
- Whether you lived free of constant financial stress

Money is just the tool.

Freedom is the goal.

A Final Reflection: What Will You Choose?

- Will you choose **status**—or **freedom**?
- Will you choose **ego**—or **humility**?
- Will you choose **short-term excitement**—or **long-term progress**?

Because in the end, money isn't about money. It's about how you live.

Table – The Five Truths of Money

Truth	**Core Lesson**
Less Ego, More Wealth	Humility builds wealth
Money Buys Time, Not Things	Time > Stuff
Survival > Brilliance	Avoid ruin
Behavior Beats Math	Reasonable > Rational
The Long Game Wins	Compounding over decades

Conclusion – Confessions

This book began with stories about money. But really, it's a book about **you and me**.

I've spent years thinking about money—not because I'm obsessed with getting rich, but because I'm obsessed with **what money allows us to do.**

I want to end with a confession:

I don't have everything figured out.

And neither does anyone else.

Why I Wrote This

I didn't write this book because I've mastered money. I wrote it because I've made **mistakes**.

- I've chased investments I didn't understand.
- I've compared myself to people I had no business comparing myself to.

- I've been too greedy, too fearful, too confident.

And each mistake taught me something I couldn't have learned any other way.

Confession 1: I'm Not the Smartest Investor

I don't beat the market every year. I don't try. What I try to do is **avoid big mistakes and stay in the game long enough to let time do the heavy lifting.**

If there's one thing I've learned, it's this: **you don't have to be brilliant to do well with money—you just have to avoid doing dumb things for long enough.**

Confession 2: I Value Boring

For years, I thought wealth was exciting. Now, I think wealth is **boring**.

- Saving every month is boring.

- Driving an old car is boring.
- Not checking your stock portfolio every day is boring.

But boring is what works.

The reward for boring?

A life that's anything but.

My Financial Philosophy

Let me share the rules that guide my decisions. They are simple, but they work for me:

1. Live Below Your Means

I don't care how much I earn—what matters is how much I keep.

Spending less than I earn gives me **freedom**.

2. Keep Room for Error

I assume things will go wrong.

Not because I'm pessimistic, but because I know I can't predict everything.

3. Avoid Debt That Could Ruin Me

Debt can be useful. But for me, **freedom is more valuable than leverage.**

4. Respect Luck and Uncertainty

I know I'm not fully in control. Luck plays a role. Timing plays a role. This keeps me humble.

5. Save for Flexibility, Not for Things

Every dollar I save is a vote for **control of my time.**

What Money Can't Do

Money can buy a lot of things, but here's what I've learned it **can't** do:

- It can't make people respect you.
- It can't make you immune to bad luck.
- It can't fix a bad marriage, bad friendships, or bad priorities.

Money can give you options, but it can't give you purpose.

What Money Can Do

What it can do—if used well—is give you:

- **Time.** The most valuable asset of all.
- **Peace.** The ability to sleep without stress.
- **Flexibility.** The freedom to say no.

Why I Hope You Ignore Most Advice (Including Mine)

Money advice can be useful—but it can also be dangerous if it doesn't fit your life.

- Your goals are different.
- Your risk tolerance is different.
- Your story is different.

Take what works. Leave what doesn't.

Your Game, Not Mine

This is your game.

The best I can do is help you think differently about it.

The Single Biggest Lesson

If you remember nothing else from this book, remember this:

Financial success has little to do with knowledge and a lot to do with behavior.

- Spend less than you earn.
- Save consistently.

- Avoid ruin.
- Give yourself time.

And be kind to yourself when you make mistakes. Because you will.

Looking Ahead

You will:

- Change your mind.
- Experience surprises.
- Regret some decisions.

And that's okay.

The goal is not perfection.

The goal is resilience.

An Invitation

As you close this book, ask yourself:

- What does "enough" look like for me?
- What kind of life do I want to design?
- What can money make possible that nothing else can?

Then build toward that. Quietly. Consistently. Humbly.

The Ending (That's Really a Beginning)

This is the end of the book, but it's the start of your story.

I don't know what the markets will do.

I don't know what the economy will do.

I don't know what surprises life has for you.

But I do know this:

If you can control your behavior, stay humble, and focus on building a life that gives you control over your time, you'll be rich—whether or not anyone else ever knows it.

Thank you for spending your time with these pages. Now go spend your money—and your life—on what matters most to you.

Table – Final Confessions

Confession	Why It Matters
I'm not brilliant	You don't need to be either
I value boring	Boring is the secret
I live below my means	Freedom > Flexibility
I keep room for error	Survive > Predict

Confession	**Why It Matters**
I respect luck	Humility keeps you safe

Epilogue

Imagine this.

It's twenty years from today.

You've lived by a simple set of rules—not perfectly, but consistently:

- You spent less than you earned.
- You saved steadily, even when it was boring.
- You avoided big mistakes and stayed in the game.
- You refused to play anyone else's game but your own.

You didn't get every decision right. You didn't need to.

And now, without even realizing it, you've built something extraordinary.

A Life That Feels Different

One morning you wake up and notice that your life just… feels lighter.

You have options:

- If you want to work, it's because you choose to—not because you have to.
- If you want to walk away from something that no longer fits, you can.
- If you want to take a risk, you know that one failure won't ruin you.

This is the quiet, unspoken goal of every page you just read.

Not a number in an account.

Not a fancy title.

Just **freedom.**

What Twenty Years of Patience Buys You

Over twenty years, compounding does something that looks almost like magic.

- The savings you thought were small grow into a cushion you never imagined.
- The decisions that once felt modest—driving a simpler car, resisting lifestyle inflation, avoiding high-interest debt—add up to a fortune of freedom.
- The fear that once kept you awake at night begins to fade.

It wasn't one giant win that changed everything. It was hundreds of small, good decisions, repeated for two decades.

Looking Back, It Wasn't About Money

When you look back on the last twenty years, you realize:

The money was never the point.

It was about:

- Buying time with your family.
- Buying flexibility to do work you enjoy.
- Buying back your peace of mind.

The accounts, the assets, the net worth—all of those things are just tools.

The real reward is how it **feels** to have control over your own life.

Your Future Self Will Thank You

You can't see it now, but your future self is standing twenty years ahead, waiting for you.

They are:

- Calmer
- Kinder
- More present

Why? Because you gave them the gift of financial independence—not wealth for its own sake, but wealth that allowed them to choose how to live.

The Small Decisions That Build a Big Life

Looking forward, ask yourself:

- Could I save a little more today?
- Could I avoid a risk that might ruin me?
- Could I say no to something I don't need, so I can say yes to something that matters later?

The answer doesn't have to be perfect.

It just has to be **better, most of the time, for a long time.**

You Don't Need Permission

You don't need a degree in finance.

You don't need to predict the market.

You don't need permission from anyone.

You just need to start.

Where to Start

- **Start with one month of expenses saved.**
- **Start with one decision to avoid showing off.**
- **Start with one plan to invest consistently.**

One small choice leads to another.

And in twenty years, you'll be astonished by how far those small choices took you.

What Happens If You Do Nothing?

Of course, you could do nothing.

You could spend everything, copy others, take big risks, and hope for the best.

Twenty years from now, you'll have a different life, too:

- A life of reacting instead of choosing.
- A life of stress instead of freedom.
- A life shaped by everyone else's priorities instead of your own.

That's the difference.

Not rich vs. poor.

But **choice vs. no choice.**

Final Words

If there's one thing I hope this book has shown you, it's that **ordinary people can do extraordinary things with money if they are patient and intentional.**

The person who looks average on the outside but quietly applies these lessons for twenty years will end up living a life that looks extraordinary on the inside.

And the best part?

You can start today.

Twenty Years from Now…

…when someone asks you the secret, you'll smile and say:

"I wasn't smarter. I wasn't luckier.

I just gave myself time. And that made all the difference."

www.ingramcontent.com/pod-product-compliance
Lightning Source LLC
Chambersburg PA
CBHW031338230926
51848CB00002B/293
9782604084624